GOD

End-time Updates
The Bride of My Son

Anthony A Eddy

BookWhip

Front and Rear Covers

An End-time Baptism in The Jordan River— The Holy Land
Refer Item: Multitudes within The Bride (P 98)

Copyright and Publishing

Printed in the United States of America

Soft Cover ISBN: 978-1-950596-29-4
Hard Cover ISBN: 978-1-950596-30-0
Ebook ISBN: 978-1-950596-31-7

12. "GOD End-time Updates The Bride of My Son"

www.thewebsiteofthelord.org.nz

Prepared on a 27in iMac™© with the use of Nisus®© Writer Pro. All trademarks™ and intellectual rights remain the property of their respective owners.

To order additional copies of this book, contact:
Bookwhip
1-855-339-3589
https://www.bookwhip.com

GOD End-time Updates

The Father offers the families of The Bride of His Son the wisdom of the centuries,
The understanding of the end-time of both salvation and redemption,
The significance of both to lives within His family:
Where truth surveys with validation.

The Bride of My Son

The coming Bride of The Son impacts fully on The Father-in-law to be,
Will fulfil all the waiting generations subject to the promise;
In yielding to, and preparing, the purity required,
For the wedding feast of The Lamb.

Anthony A Eddy

(Scribe)

Contents— Order Received

Contents— Alphabetical

Contents— Category

I, The Lord Jesus

The End-time Testimonies of God

And I hear The Lord Jesus saying,
"I,
The Lord Jesus,
beget the will of The Father in the end-time leading into mercy and relief.

I,
The Lord Jesus,
release the bound and the fixated,
release the tried and the true,
release the grateful and the inspired.

I,
The Lord Jesus,
release all into The Father's care,
into The Father's beckoning and call,
into The Father's counselling and testimony,
into The Father's honouring within My garden of eternity.

I,
The Lord Jesus,
celebrate with The Father the coming wedding of The Lamb.

I,
The Lord Jesus,
rejoice with the populace,
rejoice with the guests,
rejoice with the residents,
rejoice at large with all who would like to join in the festivities of the day.

I,
The Lord Jesus,
bring memories to the fore,
bring images of recollection,
bring the past into the present which still awaits the future.

I,
The Lord Jesus,
know My Spirit is attending on My behalf,
know He is at home and at ease,
know He is secure and enjoying all which has come to be.

I,
The Lord Jesus,
recall all which My Spirit has achieved within the days of man,
all which My Spirit has achieved within the eternity of Heaven,
foresee all which is now coming to fruition,
now coming to accountability,
now coming to the bema of which they have been warned yet have chosen to ignore.

I,
The Lord Jesus,
can hear the coming nattering of the teeth of man now in fear and trepidation,
can hear the gnashing of the teeth now expressing anger and defiance unto the summation of their life within mortality.

I,
The Lord Jesus,
assess and welcome or reject if repentance is not present on their path to grace.

I,
The Lord Jesus,
highlight and shine upon the beauty of The Earth:
upon the beauty as created,
upon the beauty as achieved,
upon the beauty as a tribute to The Father.

I,
The Lord Jesus,
will dress My church in glory as befits those enjoined with God,
will dress My church in glory with the robes of The Lamb,
with the salvation gowns of Life,
with the gowns befitting the enrobing of The Kings and Queens of God.

I,
The Lord Jesus,
am present at the parades of My People,
at their gathering and their dispersing,
at their standing and rejoicing.

I,
The Lord Jesus,
encourage and do not scorn,
uplift and do not victimize,
celebrate and do not disparage.

I,
The Lord Jesus,
have a time line for the restoration of Justice on The Earth,
have a time line for the chaining of Satan and his followers,
have a time line for a coronation with the claiming of a throne.

I,
The Lord Jesus,
have a time line for My banner,
for My Flag,
for My Standard,
for The Colours of The King;
for as such were imparted so they are prepared to fly,
shall so be flown,
from the ramparts and/or the bounds of The Edifice of God.

I,
The Lord Jesus,
attend to chaperones for the at risk and the nervous,
for the inexperienced and the insecure,
for the young and the infirm.

I,
The Lord Jesus,
invite the lost into the courtyards of God,
invite those who feel they belong to the god-forsaken—
are in need of a change in their beliefs—
for there are no God-forsaken whom God abandons or deserts.

I,
The Lord Jesus,
stipulate for My Spirit to endow,
stipulate a time frame within mortality as progress is being measured,
stipulate the absenting of sin within My Bride-in-waiting:
prior to inclusion or participation,
at a wedding with its feast.

I,
The Lord Jesus,
have a welcome planned,
have a welcome which will make up for a long time absent as calculated by man,
have a welcome with the attendance of all the Hosts of Heaven and those who
dwell therein.

I,
The Lord Jesus,
have huge anticipatory expectations of the coming eternal journeying:
with the multitudes and all My People as gathered by the centuries.

I,
The Lord Jesus,
expect and think,
expect and know,
expect and add to My Spirit's responsibilities.

I,
The Lord Jesus,
keep the tearful tearless,
keep the scared at ease,
keep the wide-eyed and uncertain at home within the family of God.

I,
The Lord Jesus,
am present so to second:
the end-time seating or kneeling at communion,
the end-time configuration of the fidgeting as seated within the fields
of inattention,
the end-time wisdom as discussed at the tables of the wise.

I,
The Lord Jesus,
know the Father's interest in all that is said and done,
in all that is carried and developed,
in all which is polished anew within the sunlight of
the morning and the moonlight of the dusk.

I,
The Lord Jesus,
know The Father's favourite subject,
the one which always gets attention,
the one which always gathers followers who choose to
stay at large within The Kingdom of The Son."

"For as the wind blows so the dust will settle."

My Content Study Aid

Introduction

These Divine texts mostly consist of Truth Statements intermixed with counselling and are presented for serious contemplation as to their ramifications and how we approach them in the conclusions we may draw. For they are filled with great significance for these present times.

I testify here to one and all that these texts are not of my writing nor instigation. These texts do not stand alone but smoothly build on the preceding ones as if designed as an unfolding story with an establishing foundation. On the original individual documents the scribe has begun each Divine call with the words: 'And I hear The Lord Jesus saying,' "...". It does not appear necessary to have this phrase repetitively introducing each call in this book. Please take it, therefore, as a 'given' as to the stated origin both by testimony and by claim.

The style of the book preserves the scribal comments in italics; while double quotation marks " " denote and enclose text of a Divine origin. British spelling is used for reasons of national culture. Layout simplifies ease of reading and personal study. Each call itself may be accurately searched from within His website. A concordance or a thesaurus has not been used at any stage prior to, during, or after the receiving of these texts. A dictionary (Oxford Concise™) has sometimes been used to comprehend fully, the words of the Divine voice used in expressing His intent. Because the texts have been received via dictation spoken by the Divine voice directly into the mind, the punctuation is subject to human interpretation. Occasionally however, when required for clarity or emphasis, the capitalisation of words, together with the paragraphing, have also been indicated by the Divine. Minor spelling 'typos' are scribal and the punctuation, together with the titles, usually are, but not always. Multiple subject matters sometimes occur in a particular call which precludes the call's naming being entirely appropriate with respect to descriptive accuracy. There are nine parts within the series which The Lord has named 'The End-time Psalms of God'. These may probably be better known by man in his naming as 'The End-time Homilies of God' - in being 'Religious discourses which are intended primarily for spiritual education rather than doctrinal instruction'.

Attached to the end of most items is 'My Content Study Aid' inserted at the request of The Lord Jesus to enhance the benefits found in meditating on and understanding the 'Hows' and 'Whys' of the truth statements and His counselling as found herein. If no such Study Aid exists at the end of an item then there are additional Journaling & Notes pages provided in the Appendix. Please remember this is your book to use in the way which best serves your growth within the discipleship of God.

Great care has been taken to ensure scribal accuracy in hearing and transcribing what are now these printed pages of Divinely originated texts. Every word is as received without later omissions, additions, substitutions or edits. May The Holy Spirit so testify as such to every enquiring soul.

The Scribe,
Hamilton, New Zealand

Wisdom of The Centuries

The End-time Testimonies of God

And I hear God The Father saying,
"The wisdom of the centuries lies at the footstool of God.

The wisdom of the centuries is waiting to be uplifted by man,
is waiting to not be seen as being vulnerable to the gathering of dust,
is waiting for the realization of wisdom's use in serving the tongue of My Son's people,
and of man as he comes to Faith.

The wisdom of the centuries accrues as it is sought,
as requests are received,
as it is downloaded in the company of The Tongues of Heaven.

The wisdom of the centuries builds as it is imparted,
builds as it is assimilated,
builds as it is adopted into the life patterns of the tongues of man.

The wisdom of the centuries should not be confused with a hula-hoop going round and round,
should not be drawn from the ethics of man,
should not be a composite just serving milk without the meat.

The wisdom of the centuries should be drawn from the well which serves up The Living Water,
should be within reach of the river wherein The Living Water flows,
should be in companionship with The Gift of Tongues so both can be received to so grow together.

The wisdom of the centuries has been nurtured in the heavens,
has been kept undefiled,
is shared with man upon a prayer request:
which can prove to be a landmark in the life of man.

The wisdom of the centuries melds his tongue with lips and vocal cords:
so all three achieve full fluency of expression.

The wisdom of the centuries neither attacks nor retreats;
is there to yield the truth in circumstances where the lies of man are present,
is there to overcome the false impressions as designed to be left in place,
is there to superimpose the wisdom of The Living God:
with all its bluntness and directness on the problems of the day and night.

The wisdom of the centuries celebrates acknowledgement,
celebrates the positioning and the successes as the white within the black and white,
celebrates in readiness for an initial fluctuating impression as it is gathered and unfolded,
yet soon competes from strength.

The wisdom of the centuries is not easily attained,
is not easily classified,
is not easily put into practice
until the tongue is fully equipped,
until the tongue is fluent,
until the tongue has practised and is enabled
to present the vowels and consonants,
without a stammer or a stutter,
as the syllables are processed for enunciation.

The wisdom of the centuries is recognized when such is heard,
is recognized when it is gifted,
is recognized when encountered against poorly thought out streams of speech.

The wisdom of the centuries is concise yet definitive,
is condensed yet complete,
is considered yet non-arguable.

The wisdom of the centuries is not subject to pre-emption,
is not subject to blasphemy,
is not subject to idolatry.

The wisdom of the centuries is often obvious when spoken,
raises eyebrows at the thoughts revealed,
silences while matters are considered as to the best way forward.

The wisdom of the centuries is often brief and restrained,
is often precise and all inclusive,
is often circumspect and honouring.

The wisdom of the centuries is not regurgitated nonsense,
is well thought out and not obscure,
is uncompromising and direct,
is positive and enhancing of the thoughts before the table.

The wisdom of the centuries is consolidated and stands firm,
is sustaining of the truth in laying waste the lies,
is supportive of endeavours based on righteousness in all its many aspects.

The wisdom of the centuries is mature and well-defined,
is sensitive to both time and space,
is consistent with The Ways of God.

The wisdom of the centuries does not violate the vows of honouring,
can upset the curses of antiquity,
can impeach immorality when encountered,
is not concerned with the ethics of man wherever or whenever they arise.

The wisdom of the centuries prevails and is not lost,
is instated and remains,
is implanted and expands.

The wisdom of the centuries is not circuitous in application,
is not disdainful in appearance,
is not a propounder of methods out of date.

The wisdom of the centuries is a gift from God,
is an enlightening of speech,
is the summation of the best,
is the containment of the worst,
is the victory of expression.

The wisdom of the centuries is an expansion of vocabulary."

My Content Study Aid

The Thunderbolts of God

The End-time Testimonies of God

And I hear God The Father saying,
"The thunderbolts of God are for the benefit of man.

The thunderbolts of God are the catechisms of the heavens,
are the wakeup calls to man,
are the sequestering of fire.

The thunderbolts of God are the fishing trips for man,
are the missionaries from heaven,
are the archetypes for the seeking of attention.

The thunderbolts of God are the reminders of the supremacy of God,
are the incubators of release,
are the instillers of respect,
are the hunters and the gatherers,
are the seesaws of the heavens.

The thunderbolts of God indicate the way stations of The Lord,
the erupting of the charges,
the cannoning of God.

The thunderbolts of God are the synthesizers of the clashes,
are the boundaries of the layers,
are the scavengers and the dumpers of the skies.

The thunderbolts of God are His protective covering over His creation,
are His preemptive strikes before defences are in play,
are His arrowheads of assault flying straight and true.

The thunderbolts of God are His agents of defence,
are His agents of attack,
are His agents of supervision in the balancing of The Earth.

The thunderbolts of God can be neutralized within the skies,
get everyone's attention when aimed at earthing on The Earth,
get everyone's attention when triggering a rainstorm as a
deluge on The Earth.

The thunderbolts of God are His weapons of fearsome fire held in reserve,
held in restraint,
held in abeyance,
in serving the wrath of God declared.

The thunderbolts of God can meet head-on and bounce,
can meet head-on and trigger,
can meet head-on and transfer,
can meet head-on in absorption,
can meet head-on and explode,
can meet in termination and demolish.

The thunderbolts of God are the positive transmitters of energy released,
strike the negative to equate to zero,
leaves the ozone in disarray,
converts the gases into compounds for absorption in the rain.

The thunderbolts of God harness the free energy of the sun as the condenser of The Earth.

The thunderbolts of God discharge the accumulations of an excess,
discharge to a lower state of readiness,
discharge so both can be stable and at rest.

The thunderbolts of God are electro-static storage pots looking for a place to land,
travel quickly across the skies while searching for a kindred
spirit to engage,
to merge with,
to be assimilated by,
the hungry and the thirsty with no place to stay:
yet with a mat of welcome on display.

The thunderbolts of God know and travel the pathways to redemption,
the pathways to attractants,
the pathways to the grasping and the seizing.

The thunderbolts of God do not travel with a fizzle,
do not travel until exhausted,
do not travel to match like with like.

The thunderbolts of God travel to meet the opposites,
travel to eliminate the opposites,
travel to forestall the building-up of an even bigger bang.

The thunderbolts of God nod their heads and say it's time to go,
open with several salvoes,
close when all is spent and finally at ease.

The thunderbolts of God can rattle the windows of man in passing,
can invade the wiring of man:
to shut the circuits down with just scorch marks to the fore,
to open up an inferno in the making which burns until
surroundings are exhausted,
or found to be just out of reach.

The thunderbolts of God can be polished and trapped by man,
when encountering an arc-way to plastic rubberised
lead-lined and lead-finned tanks,
of acidified water with large heating elements enclosed:
in a parallel linking of design with an accepting aerial
signal in the sky,
as voltage is invited to be progressively reduced,
as lead-ins are encountered,
as capacitors are so scaled.

The thunderbolts of God can be threat-controlled by man,
can be advantage-captured by man,
can be battery-stabilized by man,
can be loaded and then control-released.

The thunderbolts of God are but a Van de Graaff machine in action.

The thunderbolts of God can be items of fear and dread,
can be items of amazement and applauding.

The thunderbolts of God give rise to echos in the mountains with the rolling thunder.

The thunderbolts of God can bring children to the windows,
can awaken the sleepers in the night,
can call the witnesses to assemble before the wild fire of
the heavens.

The thunderbolts of God can be met head-on by the enemies of God,
can be met head-on in a battle with the tanks of man,
can be met head-on in a battle with the fire of man.

The thunderbolts of God can be aroused and called to serve on the battlefield of God:
against the evil foe of man,
against the satanic hordes,
against those instated and encountered,
to their dismay and detriment."

My Content Study Aid

The Functioning of Heaven

The End-time Testimonies of God

And I hear God The Father saying,
"The functioning of heaven sees The Father's Will prevail.

The functioning of heaven knows the future from the past,
knows the life within the present,
knows all aspects of eternity,
knows the grave sleepers with their tribute safely stored away.

The functioning of heaven is in tune with the orchestrations of heaven,
with the upbeat of purity,
with the downbeat of truth,
with the notes of continuum associated with both
praise and worship.

The functioning of heaven is smooth in being without unexpected interruptions,
in being without futuristic demands,
in being without implicit hesitations in requesting
revelations from the past.

The functioning of heaven is motivated by,
is within,
is guided by,
the bounds of righteousness.

The functioning of heaven knows the seat of justice so to be soon deployed in
the company of mercy.

The functioning of heaven knows the timing of the coming termination of both
grace and faith,
knows the rearrangement of The Earth,
knows the capitulations of the sovereigns,
the monarchs,
the emperors of The Earth,
knows those who will choose to fight to defend the
unjust holding of power and of authority,
knows those who would spill much blood of the innocent:
before surrendering to the inevitable.

The functioning of heaven is autonomous,
has infrastructure well established and placed,
has abilities and capabilities still unknown upon The Earth
of man.

The functioning of heaven gathers in and accumulates the bodies souls and spirits
of man,
upon a death scene due of honouring,
upon a place reserved within the Lamb's book of Life,
upon a death scene complete with angels testifying of
how the soul with Freewill,
had been applied and recorded in righteousness of morality.

The functioning of heaven always operates in the light,
has in itself no time of darkness,
has no time at all unless in a linking with the time frame of
The Earth.

The functioning of heaven raises the speculation of man,
raises the guesswork and the suppositions,
raises the objections based on ignorance,
of disbelief,
of denial of The God of Life and of Love,
of the presence of blasphemy as it issues from the tongue
and lips to let procrastination carry all away,
from any possible relationship with God.

The functioning of heaven sees angels blocking ears as the mouth of man runs free,
sees angels closing eyes at the behaviours of two upon a bed
of man,
where self-gratification arises as a curse.

The functioning of heaven is the recording venue for activities upon The Earth,
is the reference point for every seat of Justice with access to heaven,
is the maintaining of the library of man with all his deeds and actions,
with all his acts of violence and of hate,
with all his shameful acts as intermingled
with his lies and subterfuge,
where the cameras are always absent unless used as the means
of illicit control,
where pornography is rampant and goodwill has long fled the
opened stable doors of the white horse.

The functioning of heaven is overseen by The Father,
is laid out by The Father,
is determined by The Father.

The functioning of heaven has The Father judging testimonies for their content and belief
structure when heard by The Son.

The functioning of heaven is no longer damaged directly by the activities of Satan,
knows such activities are fast coming to an end,
knows the timing for the application of the shackles and
consignment to the settlement with the lake of fire.

The functioning of heaven is in the patterning of God.

The functioning of heaven is in accord with His declarations,
with His revelations,
with His proclamations through His prophets and His scribes.

The functioning of heaven is in accord and as described within the picturing there for
man within The Bible,
so man may understand the concepts and the analogies,
the metaphors and the similes,
the contrasts and the conflicts
between both good and evil:
of how the latter came to be,
of how it is to be overcome.

The functioning of heaven has had a midpoint bringing change unto the law of
the old testament,
has had a change of salvation and redemption,
of reconciliation born of sacrifice,
of movements in position by The Father,
The Son,
and The Holy Spirit,
as the priesthood set apart for serving a nation with a temple,
witnessed the temple cloth rent in two and then
to be destroyed as foretold by The Son,
as a priesthood nation misjudged and failed to recognize
their Messiah:
He whom they still await,
as the gentile bodies of The Saints of God became the temples
of new life wherein the Holy Spirit attended,
and so dwells,
in bringing forth a personal and growing relationship with God
while within mortality,
yet with an eye now firmly fixed on the personal prospect of
life sustained for eternity,
within the family of God."

My Content Study Aid

Christmas Day in Heaven

The End-time Testimonies of God

And I hear God The Father saying,
"Christmas day in heaven is a day to be duly honoured from the past of man.

Christmas day in heaven is a day enjoined for the overseeing of communion among The Saints on Earth,
is a day ultimately resulting in a commitment to the greatest sacrifice on The Earth,
is a day which led to the redemption of man from the sin within My Son's garden in Eden.

Christmas day in heaven came to be celebrated as the complete forgiveness of each repentant heart of man,
within the to be installed grace of God.

Christmas day in heaven is the launch date set for man's reconciliation with his God.

Christmas day in heaven opens the door for the fulfilment of the law.

Christmas day in heaven opens an awareness of The Freewill of man:
to be exercised within the bounds of accountability.

Christmas day in heaven opens wide the pathway to the honouring of the destiny of choice;
which negates the respecting of the default.

Christmas day in heaven leads to the days of Pentecost,
leads to the gifts of The Spirit,
leads to fluency within The Tongues of Heaven,
leads to a close and personal relationship with The Son of God,
leads to the formation of The Temples of His Spirit wherein His Spirit is now seen to dwell.

Christmas day in heaven leads to My Son's proxy ministries within The Saints of God,
authorised and empowered to declare the healing prayers as end-time healing agents of The Lord.

Christmas day in heaven is remembered by all the hosts of heaven,
by all the guardian angels,
by all the comforting angels,
by all the messaging angels.
by all the serving angels.

Christmas day in heaven left a noted absence waiting to be refilled,
left a noted absence as The Son departed on His grand
overseas experience,
left a noted absence until He dramatically returned with the
experience of a lifetime;
within mortality on The Earth of man.

Christmas day in heaven is not a recurring celebration as it is on Earth.

Christmas day in heaven is a markup day in the historical records of The Earth,
is an instigator of events which led to a new covenant in place,
is the verifiable record of all which followed in the footsteps of
The Son of God.

Christmas day in heaven signals its receipt upon The Earth,
has attributed an amazing amount of gratitude and thankfulness,
has a feedback loop which carries the reports
of homage and of love,
of praise and of worship,
of consolidation and expansion,
of bravery and forgiveness,
of assaults and depredations.

Christmas day in heaven sees the results 'of going into all the world' among The Gentile
Nations of The Earth.

Christmas day in heaven registers the paucity of acceptance among The Tribes of Israel,
registers the lack of recognition of The Messiah among The
Leaders of The Faith,
registers the restraints on the people in the days of Roman rule.

Christmas day in heaven remembers all the martyrs arising from His birth and ministry,
recognizes them in the places of highest honour with their
gowns of life and their faith intact.

Christmas day in heaven honours all who died in service to The Kingdom of God,
honours all who fell under the force of evil,
under the force of injustice,
under the force of the deceit of lies,
under the force of idolatry and barbarism
in action.

Christmas day in heaven has a schedule set for reflection,
has a schedule set for mourning,
has a schedule set for enlightenment and growth,
has a schedule set for The Empowering Edifices of God as they
spread across the landscaped nations of man.

Christmas day in heaven was instated by The Father,
saw Him shed the tears of a father,
at seeing His son so mistreated as an innocent in the hands of
the guilty,
as His priesthood holders bent and swayed the truth with the
crowd shouters for Barabbas.

Christmas day in heaven holds fast the stakes as set by developed examples of man's evil
use of his Freewill,
as injustice ruled the day,
as Barabbas was freed,
as The Messiah of The Jews was turned
into a stand-in,
for crucifixion on a cross at Calvary.

I,
The Father,
watched in the most extreme of mental anguish and waited,
with the heavens open,
as My Son was nailed and hung and suffered,
even to expiry unto death.

Christmas day in heaven initiated the tasking of Jesus upon The Earth of man,
initiated the lines of persecution and the lines of forgiveness,
as I,
The Father,
became a spectator at the death of My Son.

Christmas day in heaven resulted in a testimony of life over death,
resulted in the resurrection of My Son,
resulted in the two commandments of The Lord,
resulted in the disciples with faith and commitment
being welcomed,
as The Bride of Christ,
into My Son's garden of life within eternity."

My Content Study Aid

The Season of Iniquity

The End-time Testimonies of God

And I hear God The Father saying,
"The season of iniquity is now upon The Earth,
is spreading like the plague,
is attempting to forestall,
to frustrate,
The End-time Works of God.

The season of iniquity witnesses language becoming coarse,
respect being lost,
anger becoming dominant,
as man throws himself down a slippery slope on which he cannot stop.

The season of iniquity is arousing The Wrath of God The Father.

The season of iniquity speaks of crime sprees running wild,
speaks of criminal non-accountability,
speaks of the leg roping of the enforcers of the law,
speaks of the carrying of guns for supposed self-defence.

The season of iniquity witnesses an intensification of free-flowing violence,
of much broken glass,
of much burning of the cars within the streets,
of much plundering and theft,
of much injury with hospitalization to the fore,
of much vindictiveness asserted upon the
innocent and the helpful.

The season of iniquity witnesses much throwing and ducking,
much tear gas wafting in the air,
much water being squirted at the recalcitrant and unruly.

The season of iniquity lingers with its time of wayward behaviour,
lingers with its time of antisocial reactions,
lingers with its time as spent within the grounds of the
correction facilities.

The season of iniquity sees the bending and the breaking,
sees the scorching and the burning,
sees the robberies and the losses.

The season of iniquity is peppered with the lies,
is salted with deceit.

The season of iniquity sees the invaders of the self-help stores
stripping and stealing,
sampling and casting,
tasting and strewing far and wide,
without regret or an apology,
for what is being trampled underfoot.

The season of iniquity is not the drinkers' paradise,
is not the sacking of what is perceived to be of value,
is not the raiding of the cool stores or the liquor stores at large.

The season of iniquity does not highlight the inebriated as the ringleaders of first choice.

The season of iniquity is the realization of the schemers and the fraudsters:
taking an overriding interest in creating mayhem,
for the well being of the collective with no pride in ownership,
with no fear of repercussions,
with no fear of arrest among
the unruly and the violent.

The season of iniquity is not a time for the appearance of the women,
for the presence of the women,
for the participation of the women:
within the flinging and the tossing,
the shattering and the cracking,
the lifting and the taking.

The season of iniquity sees the torching of the burnable,
sees the opportunistic ram-raiding of the jewellers,
sees the creation of a mess.

The season of iniquity is a field day for the irresponsible,
for those with an imagined score to settle;
is a field day for the negative viewpoints attacking life itself;
is a field day for the gangs and the drug dealers
with the hot wiring of the preferred vehicles of choice,
with the snatching of the purses and the weaponry as carried.

The season of iniquity overloads the ability of righteousness to cope,
overcomes the weapons of insignificance,
overcomes the reporting of the truth,
overcomes those succumbing to the lies.

The season of iniquity experiences the ransacking of the homes,
the hammering on the doors,
the sound of breaking glass,
the throwing of molotov cocktails through the windows,
without a care as to the landing places.

The season of iniquity is void of responsibility,
is void of accountability,
is void of any areas of concern,
as the masses crowd and loot,
as the masses gather and run riot,
as the masses trumpet their successes throughout
the day and the night.

The season of iniquity feeds upon the jealousy of false achievements,
feeds upon the scent of blood,
feeds upon the accidents of injury and pain.

The season of iniquity removes the smiles from faces,
removes the handshakes from society,
removes the hugs and the congratulations from the sports fields
and the sporting endeavours of man.

The season of iniquity rubbishes the cry for help,
ignores the relationship of friends,
fails to recognize the assuredness of a blood relationship.

The season of iniquity witnesses the breakdown of society,
the pawing at the pawnshop,
the emptying of wallets,
the closing of industry where the losses are too great.

The season of iniquity verifies the stamp of evil,
verifies the evil intent,
verifies the casting out onto the pavement of a tenant in arrears.

The season of iniquity lasts until the burnout of the selfish attitudes,
lasts until the changing of the seasons,
lasts until exhaustion brings relief from rampaging with
the rioters,
lasts until the weather stops berating the homeless and the poor.

The season of iniquity views a broken city,
views the death knells of the structures of the rich,
views the wreckage of the structures of the trampled and forlorn."

My Content Study Aid

____

____

____

____

The Catching of A Breath

The End-time Testimonies of God

And I hear God The Father saying,
"The catching of a breath is often overlooked,
is often out of time,
is often surplus and not needed on the scene.

The catching of a breath can be a reflex action,
can be a measure of alarm,
can be just prior to a call for help.

The catching of a breath can be a reaction to what the eyes do see,
to what the ears to hear,
to what the skin does feel,
to what is in the air.

The catching of a breath often follows the surroundings breeding fear,
the surroundings of release.

The catching of a breath is the emergency opening of the airways with a gasp or gulp,
is the setting of the body to a state of alertness,
is the preparation in the shock of the possibility for the need of
either flight or fight.

The catching of a breath creates an instant evaluation to preserve the status quo.

The catching of a breath holds in expectation,
holds in readiness for action,
holds until the analysis is complete.

The catching of a breath is a short term pause within the bounds of activity,
is a stopgap measure to satisfy the senses that all is well,
is a network analysis of any urgency seeking attention.

The catching of a breath is not a yawn in action,
is not an addition to an exercising of the body,
is not a pause simply called by a distraction which diverts
without surprise.

The catching of a breath is somewhat like a reflex action
which withdraws a hand from where it may be burnt,
which shuts the eyelids in a blink in protecting the eyes from
what appears to be a too close high speed approach.

The catching of a breath shortens and speeds up when anxiety is prolonged,
when adrenaline has been initiated,
when senses are aroused and attentive.

The catching of a breath can be an expression of surprise—
as when a fish first strikes and takes the bait upon a rod,
as when a racing track has cars which rush and tumble
and bounce off one another,
as when the body senses that which was unexpected—
hot instead of cold,
cold instead of hot,
running water with a residual presence preferring
one or the other,
as it issues from a labelled tap.

The catching of a breath can be as a result of the pricking of a rose with the resultant
check for blood,
can be a peck from a bird which refuses to let go when held
within a hand,
can be the crunching on a loosened filling from a tooth,
as an unexpected gift when chewing on a sweet.

The catching of a breath is a protective ability as installed by My Son,
is a prime reactor to a sudden change in circumstance,
is a levelling out of man's senses to the playing fields of life.

The catching of a breath brings caution to the front,
brings caution not released,
sees caution to completion.

The catching of a breath signals the appearance of a difficulty,
the coming of the unexpected,
the clashing with an existing usage of the body.

The catching of a breath speaks of a break in regularity,
bequeaths a hold unto the lungs,
brings a hesitation to the cycle which leaves the air not expelled.

The catching of a breath is as the setting necessary to fire a shotgun,
at a target sought with accuracy;
is as a hunter with the rifle scope set without a quiver or a shake,
on the game as selected;
is as a camera with a low light shot when steadiness,
with the framing is the goal,
where blurring is far from the objective.

The catching of a breath hinders the diving into water,
hinders the smoker with a cough,
hinders the spotlight on the game where dog food is required.

The catching of a breath speaks of the initial acceleration of a takeoff from a runway,
speaks of the moment when the wheels are about to
re-encounter contact with The Earth.

The catching of a breath awaits the bump when a boat reaches land and the quayside
passes on the jolt.

The catching of a breath is being in a car's front passenger's seat with a doubting of the
driver's ability.

The catching of a breath is when hauling in a fish through the waves upon the shoreline,
in seeing the fish throw the hook as it flounders
on its side,
in the shallowness of the water until the next
wave sets it up for a fast escape,
as an arrowhead is drawn on the water's
surface pointing out to sea,
in confirmation of the loss.

The catching of a breath is there when a hammer wielded carelessly misses and hits the
waiting nail.

The catching of a breath is there when a long golf drive decides to end up in the rough,
when it bounces into the water,
when it rolls into the sand,
when it was driven out of bounds,
when it is online for the hole but lips it
to run on for several feet,
while laughing at its close escape.

The catching of a breath is spontaneous yet sometimes open to regret,
is lost in time yet sometimes open to applause,
is throttled by the obvious yet sometimes results in pain.

The catching of a breath is not desirable when dwelling within the sporting
prowess displayed,
or in the comforting of embarrassment elsewhere in a life."

My Content Study Aid

The Wrath of God The Father

The End-time Testimonies of God

And I hear God The Father saying,
"The wrath of God The Father is soon to fall upon The Earth.

The wrath of God The Father is soon to seek His vengeance for His treatment by man,
is soon to carry out His promises to those of no faith,
of no righteousness,
of no love for God or of His caring for The Earth.

The wrath of God The Father is to fall on the underserving of The Earth,
on the greedy and the selfish,
on the immoral and the unjustified,
on the criminals and the liars,
on the abortionists and the false teachers,
on the violent and the murderous,
on the members of the drug cartels and all who
profit from the sales leading to addiction.

The wrath of God The Father falls upon the atheists in their denials,
the agnostics who are too careless with their
mouths to sustain a testimony of My Son.

The wrath of God The Father knows the culprits and the fraudsters,
knows the cartels in business as they too rob and cheat
with overcharging,
with the fear of enforcement for lack of compliance in
bending to their wills.

The wrath of God The Father will see all such come tumbling down,
from their self-proclaimed thrones and hierarchies
of lust and unforgiveness,
of embezzlement and mistreatment,
of all the evil endeavours as operating
in the dark side of life,
of all who either knowingly,
or not,
are the slaves of Satan:
with his cohorts of disease and as the soul stealers from
the rightful owners who have lost their Freewill choice,
under Satan's subjugation.

The wrath of God The Father is about to fall on the false prophets,
on the crystal gazers,
on the star readers and all the promoters of
the new age lies and deceit,
on the astrologers and their horoscopes.

The wrath of God The Father knows the breeders of false doctrines where My Son
is not at the centre,
is neither upheld nor honoured as the only way
to eternal life within My Family:
woe to those who have made their choice in
denial of the sacrifice of My Son,
for the evidence is compiled against them in readiness for
its presenting before The Great White Throne of God.

The wrath of God The Father is real and tangible,
is physical and mortal,
is a final warning for man's existence outside the bounds
of God.

The wrath of God The Father knows the approaching closeness of the harrowing,
with the presenting shortage available to repentance
from a distinct change of heart.

The wrath of God The Father has been building over centuries,
as ageing man has continued in his turning from God
in his youth,
unto the evilness of Satan,
as the greed of man has taught him the shortcuts to success,
as the top camaraderie of the masonic lodges
have overwritten the manuscripts of God,
where the transparency of God is vanquished
down the drains of secrecy.

The wrath of God The Father has a very long memory,
knows where all the secrets are hidden,
knows for what the ill-gotten fortunes were used in the
times of expansion,
knows the foundations of the fortunes of today as carried
forward into commerce,
where the core is rotten,
where the core was never cleansed by repentance,
where the core still carries its inheritance of evil
with its misery abroad.

The wrath of God The Father will no longer tolerate an evil origin for that attempting
to reside within The Kingdom of My Son.

The wrath of God The Father will purge evilness in all its many guises,
in all its many attachments,
in all its many corrupted personnel,
in all its investments made with an evil
intent of greed and selfishness:
borne of collusion in the night.

The wrath of God The Father will not have the godlessness and the evilness of man
surface in The Kingdom of His Son.

The wrath of God The Father will overcome the devious,
the deceptive,
as the trumpeting of truth strikes out the false prophets with their lies:
from their attempts to gain legitimacy and honour within the Kingdom
of My Son,
from the illegitimate and the dishonourable edifices of man,
still attempting to be sustained by man.

The wrath of God The Father does not fall on those who have honoured
and have appreciated,
the gifts of The Spirit of My Son both at Pentecost
and in the truth of centuries which followed,
to now know where The Temples of My Son exist in
honour and in detail,
with His Spirit's gifts accompanied by
The Ark of The New Covenant,
before The Throne of Grace.

The wrath of God The Father is the end-time straightening of the record of man
in his entirety,
opens the way for the coming kingdom with The Earth prepared
in readiness,
with The Earth open to resettlement on the lands within The Will of God.

The wrath of God The Father honours the birthright of the nations,
the origin of species,
the creation works of God The Son under the
oversight of God The Father.
The God of The Earth and beyond created and handled the DNA of strangers
from beyond,
with the blending of the created DNA of man upon The Earth.

The wrath of God The Father visits to achieve His will,
visits to ensure His will is carried out,
visits to ensure justice has been done.

The wrath of God The Father has many variants available,
has many methods of delivery,
has many options of terminating the targets of destruction.

The wrath of God The Father is not subject to appeal,
is not subject to mercy when mercy has been denied,
by the usurpers of My vengeance,
is not subject to grace where there is no shadow
of repentance,
as the sneers still occupy the faces.

The wrath of God The Father does not linger on the death scenes of man,
does not linger on the causes which clashed with the will
of God,
does not linger on the closing of the record in completion
with the finality,
of all decisions bearing on the scenes and the displays
of man.

The wrath of God The Father knows of nothing which can mitigate the circumstances as
set for termination,
which can set apart the circumstances
for review,
which can reduce,
soften,
or negate the suffering as brought about
and paid for by the person in dissent.

The wrath of God The Father has a Son who was tortured before His death,
who was still being tortured during His
dying breaths,
who was seen and mocked until His dying day,
by those who should have bent the knee to Him,
to so put themselves under His command.

The wrath of God The Father falls on those who deny the ability of God to punish,
the ability of God to influence the affairs of man,
the ability of God to open the supposed non-existent gates to hell.

The wrath of God The Father is laid upon the altar of the living,
is laid at the feet of the martyrs,
is laid across the hearts of the innocent for the sharing of
the grief.

The wrath of God The Father is created by the uncaring attitudes of man,
for the signalling of the unimportance of God within their lives,
for the ignoring and the laughing at the unanswered calls of God,
upon the time and non-existent conscience circling in its emphasis,
of shouting a nil response.

The wrath of God The Father now falls with retribution,
for as man has lived and measured through the centuries,
so it will be splashed and laid before him:
as he carved so will he be carved;
as he dissected so will he be dissected;
as he was killed so will he be killed;
as he squandered all that God did offer so will he be
rejected and left as a broken shell;
as he buried alive so will the victims seek justice;
as the victims of the onslaught suffered death with a
lack of mercy,
so shall it be meted out to all who took part with mercy
being absent,
amid screams which fell on active ears,
as the flames arose in starting from within the
brushwood round the feet.

The wrath of God The Father witnesses the impaling of the high winds of the seas,
with the dismantling of the structures as the residues collapse,
to block the access ways to recovery,
the flooding of the land which washes all before with the rivers
running wild.

The wrath of God The Father knows the tsunamis,
the earthquakes with the interlocked candles of My Son,
as they flood and shake and burn all which lies within
the pathways of nature's war with man:
the landslips and the ice floes;
the collapsing of the mines and the coverings
of avalanches;
the spreading of the wild fires from the lightning
strikes of God,
which cannot be measured for intensity by
the equipment held by man,
yet leaves a fast tracking trail of destruction,
as the fire tornadoes twirl in companionship with the winds,
to carry the flames and sparks across the divides of man.

The wrath of God The Father seizes the quartering of The Earth,
the cleansing of the shorelines,
the clearance of the dockyards with the wharves
and anchorages,
at the seafronts of the river mouths.

The wrath of God The Father seizes the cleansing of the cities from the blackened hearts
of man,
knows both the physical and the electronic addresses
where the mail is far from pure,
where lies occur at will as the internet plays and gambles,
with the hearts and souls of man.

The wrath of God The Father knows the beasts of man,
knows the beasts of God,
knows how they trample and toss and stamp and kick
to remove the vice of man,
to remove the dens of darkness,
to remove the caves of strippers,
to remove the major moves of Satan in the churning
of pornography,
within the children and the youth as they dwell within mortality,
under the control of demons.

The wrath of God The Father cleans The Earth of embedded sin,
purges the bedrooms with same sexes on the beds,
clears the languages of profanities and curses,
clears the filth along the roadsides and the riverbanks,
to be gathered and bleached along the journeys of being
washed down the rivers to the open seas.

The wrath of God The Father has no value attached to the sinning souls of Satan,
who see no need to repent nor to put their hearts through
a sea change of intent,
despite the warning proximities of the prowess of God.

The wrath of God The Father is not modified,
not cancelled,
not deleted:
by the forthcoming prayers of the people of His Son attempting to
soften His stance,
upon man's ignoring the taught morality of God with man's
accompanying loss of life within mortality,
so placing man beyond the field of redeeming Grace."

My Content Study Aid

The Circumference of a Square

The End-time Testimonies of God

And I hear God The Father saying,
"The circumference of a square puts meaning to a descriptive test.

The circumference of a square transliterates a circle in the making,
transliterates concepts of geometry,
transliterates concepts known to algebra.

The circumference of a square can be the four touching points of a square within a circle,
can be the total of a bounding perimeter reached by
multiplying the length of one side by four.

The circumference of a square brings a hesitation to the theory,
brings a likely alternative for consideration,
calls for a release of that which brings constraint but
serves no purpose.

The circumference of a square is a nonsense to the informed,
is an error bred of ignorance to the uninformed.

The circumference of a square is an internal clash of terms,
is an impossibility in a face to face discussion,
is a trial of language in a serving of mathematics onto the
plates of choice.

The circumference of a square is a term of unfamiliar usage,
is a term mathematicians would only use in the making of a joke,
is a term unpolished by any likely arithmetical application to be found,
in a ground search for the truth.

The circumference of a square does not lead to advancement in a subject,
does not pose a question based on knowledge,
does not augur well for usage by a student in end of
year exams.

The circumference of a square is best avoided for discussion,
is best avoided for a heart to heart,
is best avoided when encountering a blank face,
without a trace of a smile.

The circumference of a square ties up and looses ignorance in action of the definitions,
may be of some small assistance in the studying of shapes,
may show up when testing understanding of raw input of
the day.

The circumference of a square raises no question that a perimeter enquiry on a square:
will not answer in completeness;
will not answer in particulars;
will not answer without exampled calculations.

The circumference of a square can be encumbered by an effort to go beyond the theory,
to conjecture what the question means,
to seek an answer to a question stalled
by a breakdown in the language,
where the terms are incorrectly listed and so misapplied.

The circumference of a square is unrelieved by the spirit or the soul.

The circumference of a square can seek but will not gain,
can hunt but will not find,
can question but will not receive a resolution of the query.

The circumference of a square beggars the question of intelligence,
beggars the means of application,
beggars the life of an application,
of an answer coming forth.

The circumference of a square is not set in concrete,
will not melt and run within the sunlight,
cannot be reinforced to stand alone by the rods of iron.

The circumference of a square is correctly applied to the circumference interests
of a circle,
cannot be usually defined as the area enclosed by a four-
cornered square.

The circumference of a square is semi-meaningless in intent,
is a partial misapplication of the terms involved,
is an overshoot requiring a reversal of deletion and correction.

The circumference of a square specifies very little,
leaves the doorway swinging to and fro in a draft without
any definitive meaning,
leaves the onlookers standing around with puzzled faces
and with a shoulder shrug at best.

The circumference of a square has no relationship with man,
has no relationship with God,
when in the English tongue.

The circumference of a square has no part in a game of snakes and ladders,
has no part in most games of chance,
has a small part in an effort to complete a
meaningful understanding,
has a small part in a game of monopoly where the text

upon a square,
is broken into parts and relegated to the surrounding
four edges:
for instructional display as for the reading by the players,
in their placements around the board.

The circumference of a square can contain information pertinent to the game,
can change or alleviate the rules of play in progression
round the board,
can increase or enforce a decrease in the buildings
on the properties,
from where the rent is sometimes calculated on a landing,
when a rent demand sees wealth so changing hands.

The circumference of a square can be liberated from a snow field in the centre of a town,
can leave it swept and clean,
can see the flood waters encroaching on
the circumference,
can leave the town square wet and muddy with the
receding of the waters.

The circumference of a square can reflect the inundations of the tidal sweeps,
can reflect the effects of sand storms on a flat enclosure,
of dust,
of ice,
as locations change the environments around The Earth."

My Content Study Aid

Evil on The Earth

The End-time Testimonies of God

And I hear God The Father saying,
"Evil on The Earth attempts to distract and disenchant,
attempts to seize and take possession,
attempts to discriminate and separate.

Evil on The Earth vibrates with the pulse of disparity,
with the pulse of captivity,
with the pulse of the deeds of yesterday.

Evil on The Earth strikes a pose and preens,
strikes a pose and marshals,
strikes a pose and photographs.

Evil on The Earth is the marker of iniquity,
is the marker of self-centredness,
is the marker calling for attention.

Evil on The Earth is the voyeur of the night,
is the voyeur of the childhood and the youth,
is the voyeur of the indecent and unclothed.

Evil on The Earth speaks of double-dealing,
speaks of intransigence of dishonesty,
speaks of building the bonfires of the lies.

Evil on The Earth grabs to not let go,
grasps to induce acceptance,
seizes to procure the feeding of the night.

Evil on The Earth keeps the shades of sunlight drawn,
keeps the sequestered as they are committed,
keeps history enchained within the past,
enchained within a future of enforced obedience.

Evil on The Earth recognizes a snowfall in the spring,
calls in a barrage of a recall to the winter,
imposes hardships without the keys of change.

Evil on The Earth spreads far and wide as if a disease in the making.

Evil on The Earth subjugates and commands the good into the discredited,
the good into the silent,
the good into the churlish and dissatisfied.

Evil on The Earth transforms and disfigures with the cutting of the skin,
with the inking of the sanquine,
with the piercing of extremities in emphasis,
of a standout in the culling,
of the ineptitudes of man.

Evil on The Earth has been known for centuries,
has surfaced and resurfaced as history migrated to the papered works of man.

Evil on The Earth is unchained in the midst of a war,
is unchained in the usurping of power and authority,
is unchained when money changes hands and servitude is bought.

Evil on The Earth is driven by its love of money,
is gathered by extortion,
by fraud,
by the cartels of overpricing,
by that of robbery and violence,
by the factoring of an exchange of debt.

Evil on The Earth in accumulation is secreted within a dressage of respectability,
of acceptability,
of accountability:
of casinos and the games of weighted chance,
of protection from the dangers as generated,
of the internet where identities are obscured
and escape is easy,
of the money changers as they count and shuffle,
of the drugdoms inherent in the easy money flow,
wherein the gangs are rampant as they manufacture or distribute with
the mules in tow.

Evil on The Earth surmounts the barriers of righteousness,
surmounts the technicalities of avoidance,
surmounts the truth of rectitude,
surmounts the traps for lies with the transfers of the funds
via remittances,
in the process of the settlements of debt,
or the structuring of a shell without remorse.

Evil on The Earth will I,
The Father,
stop within My wrath:
stop the seeding and the breeding;
stop the planning and the instigations;
stop the expansions and the governing.

Evil on The Earth will I,
The Father,
terminate and destroy all the kingpins and the smugglers,
all the lieutenants with their
subordinate rings,
all the cash flows and the sources.

Evil on The Earth will I,
The Father,
puncture and deflate,
apply the refiner's fire,
as I inspect and segregate the travellers of righteousness:
from the burning of the fuel,
and all from which it's sourced
or procured:
the tainted funds arising from the
lives of crime and lust.

Evil on The Earth is to be washed and bleached,
to be whitened and rinsed and dried and cleansed,
by the flood the sea the sun the rain the wind and the fire of God:
exploding to consume in the fullness of combustion.

Evil on The Earth is to condense on Satan,
is to wither in collapse as his kingdom shrinks in its surroundings,
as the people with the evil hearts dissipate and so fade away.

Evil on The Earth is tested when Satan is released,
when Satan would again attempt to arouse his kingdom.

Evil on The Earth fails the bailing of Satan for a season,
fails to explore and to uplift,
fails to satisfy or to reward,
fails to again attribute truth as a belief in lies.

Evil on The Earth is not at home in the family of God,
is not at home within the garden of The Son,
is not at home within eternal life when visiting the intergalactic
creations of God,
is not at home where fallen angels cannot exist.

Evil on The Earth has its time within the sun,
has its time within the web of man,
has its time when accountability rules and imprisons,
has its time of transference to the rubbish bins of history,
in readiness for a new beginning."

The Wonders of The World

The End-time Testimonies of God

And I hear God The Father saying,
"The wonders of the world are configured by God,
are created by God,
will not fade away within the time shield of man.

The wonders of the world are the displays of grandeur which only God can place,
on His tableau for The Saints of God.

The wonders of the world are not artificial,
are not make believe,
are not squanderers of expense.

The wonders of the world are well worth the going and the seeing,
the searching and the finding,
the voyaging and the discovering:
of all that God has composed as a tribute to The Earth.

The wonders of the world do not speak of signs,
do not speak of miracles,
speak of some things in between.

The wonders of the world do invite attention,
do invite assessment,
do invite the awe of presentation.

The wonders of the world invoke a sense of inspiration,
a sense of the marvelling at the achievements of our God,
a sense of invocation worthy of surrounding what is seen to be.

The wonders of the world are the rolling credits to the architect,
are the summations within the highlight of design,
are the surveillances worth the effort of attending,
are the travellers' delights spread around for observation.

The wonders of the world lift the scope of man's environment,
enrich the amusement arcades of God,
hold fast to the installed and the completed,
shine forth without admonishment or astonishment,
bring forth the wonders of both the night and the day as His
glory is revealed:
in His finality of the setting of the scenes of God.

The wonders of the world exist and are:
for by such are the wonders of the world declared,
for through such are the wonders of the world made known,
for in such are the wonders of the world appreciated both
within their naming,
their finding,
and forthcoming on display.

The wonders of the world are attributed to God on the basis of the beauty
endemic in His creation.

The wonders of the world are there to be noticed,
are there to absorb the interest of the committed,
of the sighted and of the hearing,
of the explorers and the investigators,
of the discoverers and the appreciative,
of all which God so placed to qualify among the secluded yet the discoverable,
the distant yet the definable,
the remote yet the viewable.

The wonders of the world bring awesome into vocabularies,
bring gazing into focussing,
bring amazement into the proximity of understanding
the majestic and the colourful,
the stationary and the travellers,
the unfolding and the moonlit,
the noisy and the attention-getters,
the rising and the setting with the
dressing of each day.

The wonders of the world should beget the curiosity of man,
should encounter the interest of man,
should include man as an intrinsic part of the beauty of this
World of God.

The wonders of the world can be viewed from nowhere else but here:
upon the third planet from the sun.

The wonders of the world are created to be seen,
are created to be heard,
are created to be visited,
are created to become the marvels of the mind.

The wonders of the world are not:
to be there but overlooked,
to be there but forsaken,
to be there but ignored;
for ignorance,

with complacency feeding procrastination,
is no defence to that which God has chosen to install,
as His innate ability to call attention to His creation,
of the majesty and the beauty now composed
for presentation within the world of man.

The wonders of the world are not difficult to discover,
are not priced to be visited,
are free for the enjoyment of all upon The Earth.

The wonders of the world encourage and enlist,
are there to be enjoined onto an approval listing compiled by
the visitors and the informed of man.

The wonders of the world are there to be expressed by the word of mouth,
are there to be discussed by the interested at the locations and
the timing,
are there to stand and testify of the presence of The God of
this world,
plus all the others within the continuum of God.

The wonders of the world are there to be cherished and adored by man:
for all which has been achieved by the landlord of The Earth,
the landlord of this world,
the landlord busied in the caring for all His invited guests
with adoption into His family as set upon The Earth,
as destined for eternity with God.

The wonders of the world decorate the palaces,
the castles,
the cathedrals,
the temples,
together with the sanctuaries —
The Edifices of God wherein My People live and grow in Grace,
with the support of The Colours of The Kingdom.

The wonders of the world vibrate with excitement at their proximity to man,
in being determined to put on their best displays
to each audience as gathered:
under the canopy of the stars or the skies of God."

My Content Study Aid

The Relationships of Man

The End-time Testimonies of God

And I hear God The Father saying,
"The relationships of man are confused and somewhat temporary.

The relationships of man are often resulting from the devil's interference,
the devil's slippery slopes,
the devil's game of hide and seek with
the emotions of the children of God.

The relationships of man are secured by attachment,
are secured by a pledge,
are secured by a vow,
are secured by a promise,
are secured by a written page,
are secured by a verbal agreement,
are secured by a life within a monastery,
are secured by a life within the church of My Son,
are secured by a very particular way of life.

The relationships of man can bloom and develop,
can cry out for release.

The relationships of man can fail for want of children,
can fail for want of money,
can fail for want of nearby neighbours,
can fail upon the mount of loneliness,
can fail within the pit of separation,
can fail upon the font requiring assimilation,
can fail in the absence of a job,
can fail in the difficulty of transportation,
can fail upon the waves and storms of the seas of life.

The relationships of man are separated by death,
are prolonged by illness,
are revived in the presence of the miracles as granted:
within the family of God,
within a close relationship of the love and trust of God,
within the prayer fields of the cognizant and sincere,
with knowledge and wisdom and experience of how to
deal with,
the vanquishing of evil from the stable it comes to call as home,
in surroundings of the curses as gathered over centuries,
with the ailments of inheritance,
in the absence of an overdue cleansing of the body soul and spirit.

The relationships of man are the most secure
when dwelling within the adopted family of God,
where the jewels and treasures of life are kept in safety on
the far side of the grave,
where the gifts of The Spirit are readily available,
where the shell of man has sought and attained conversion,
to a temple of The Lord:
where His Spirit dwells in readiness for transitioning
The Temple,
on the vacating of mortality,
into an environment of eternal life with God.

The relationships of man are numerous as increased by an education,
by a marriage,
by a holiday abroad,
by a meeting of a kindred spirit in the rough and tumble of a life,
by a time at rest where The Temple can be restored to health,
by a time of celebration where the passage of time opens up the
reason for the gathering,
as memories are resharpened,
as gratefulness is acknowledged,
as the generations are recorded for the honouring of age,
with relationships that have stood the test of time in readiness
for a call for introductions,
with an acknowledgement of well-earned status:
as mixed within the efforts of the lifetimes,
with the crops as cared for and so reaped.

The relationships of man overcome the reticence of some,
surmount the welcome hands of many,
converse with the reservoirs of knowledge.

The relationships of man are birthed from journeys of establishment,
are birthed from cyclones of independence,
are birthed from settling on reliance on Freewill.

The relationships of man are wary of the dangers which threaten life at large,
are wary of diseases and of malnutrition,
are wary of locations with no sympathy for life:
where food is scarce and difficult to produce.

The relationships of man seek a sharing of production,
seek a sharing of abilities,
seek a sharing of education,
with the vocabularies of achievement.

The relationships of man seek to know the teachers and the informed within society,
seek to know the successful as measured by their pots of gold,
seek to be acquainted with the thorough and respectful,
seek to be at ease with the familiar and the tools.

The relationships of man deserve the occupations:
which enlarge the larders;
which can provide the shelter;
which can achieve the means for the clothing of a family;
which can obtain the educations as suited to a family's objectives:
as matching the desired endeavours of the hearts;
which can surmount the difficulties if attractive items are purloined.

The relationships of man should each include a relationship with God:
a relationship as driven goalwards under the growth of righteousness and truth,
and the companionship of Freewill;
a relationship as driven towards the bounds of eternity with a family united;
a relationship as driven goalwards with the shedding of the lies,
with the vacating of the fields of sins,
with the opening of the doors and pathways leading to eternal life,
with The Father,
The Son,
and The Holy Ghost:
as a family becomes a part of The Bride of Christ with a place prepared,
in the wonders of His garden as evil is resolved and negated,
at The Great White Throne of God."

My Content Study Aid

The Secrets of The Seas

The End-time Testimonies of God

And I hear God The Father saying,
"The secrets of the seas are hidden in the behaviour of the seas.

The secrets of the seas speak of a time of peace and quiet with the settling of the seas,
speak of a time of wildness and unruliness with the arousing of the seas.

The secrets of the seas lie within the heartbeat of the seas,
the pulsating of the seas,
the surging of the seas with the tugging of the lady of encircling.

The secrets of the seas visit and relax,
build and retreat,
throb and return.

The secrets of the seas are well hidden from the sight of man,
from the knowledge base of man,
from the signals of arousal,
from the signals submitting to the ways and means of peace and harmony,
upon the surface of the waters.

The secrets of the seas lie within the waters of The Earth,
within the selected naming into oceans of location,
within the fragmentation naming prospects of the seas,
in companionship with the touching lands whereon man has made his homes.

The secrets of the seas,
as they compile the oceans,
depends on the shaping of the adjoining land masses,
of where they chose to thrust the water in its travels within the currents of the seas.

The secrets of the seas lies within the sun power as dispersed;
the wind power as submitting to the jurisdictions as encountered,
in the condensing of the sun's evaporation of the seas;
of where the mountains would obstruct
to force the shedding of the loads,
which the winds do freely carry;
the currents of the seas as the transmitters of the heating of the waters,
within the cycling as set by God.

The secrets of the seas is their stacking with abundant life forms:
fully suited to their surroundings of the dark or light,
of the deep or shallow,
of the swift or slow,
of the tumultuous or placid,
of the warm or cold,
of the rock or sand,
of the nursery or predator.

The secrets of the seas are worthwhile discovering and noting,
detail the predictable movements of the masses,
locate the food of man.

The secrets of the seas hide the controlling influences of the climate features for locations
on The Earth.

The secrets of the seas are as the sifters of the powers of might and majesty,
are as the apportioners of rain and sunlight,
are as the deliverers of:
the rainbows and the clouds,
the warmth and the frigidity,
the feasting and the starving,
the windswept and the calm.

The secrets of the seas is their reaction timing to the presenting of the influence:
of the lady of the night and of the day,
with the impressive tidal surges of invasions
and the drifting of retreats.

The secrets of the seas know the flowing of the rivers as the streamers of the seas,
as the carriers and the spreaders of
the cocktails of nutrition,
from the stockpiled and
inhospitable to the unaccustomed,
where size may be important.

The secrets of the seas bequeath and endow,
uplift and share,
give rise to very little waste,
feed its own within the shelter of its waters.

The secrets of the seas know the familiarity of the pressure spots of depth,
know the dangers fraught when surfacing as protection with
stability is lost.

The secrets of the seas know the smokers and the flamers arising from the depths,
know the tremors and the quakes as the sea is tossed and shoved,
in the turmoil of making room:
from an elbow in the stomach which sometimes springs a belch.

The secrets of the seas know how to engage a hurricane,
how to allow it to expand,
how to feed it with the water and the power as it in turn,
feeds the waves which break upon the shores,
feeds the waves as flooding reaches out to the
cities with homes and offices,
then leaving them to the cleaners,
the restorers,
and the effort of rebuilding,
in the lee of the flooding as it just chooses to depart.

The secrets of the seas is their ability to invade and wash,
is their ability to purge and cleanse the shorelines of The Earth,
to vanquish the culpable with their ability to ignore.

The secrets of the seas hide the properties which make them the attackers of the
status quo,
the instigators of the changes wrought upon the seaside
of proximity,
the destructors of the beauty as perceived to be nourished,
and extended by and through the reach of man.

The secrets of the seas are not influenced by man except for the speeding up of the runoff
from the bordered land.

The secrets of the seas are determined and set by God,
are witnessed and judged by man.

The secrets of the seas can engulf in pursuit of the dealings of man—
his encroachment of Freewill:
on the shore lines and the flood plains,
the harbours and the river mouths,
where man has built the stopbanks for protection,
from the water laying claim afresh to all the land which has
been claimed,
and used within the past,
with the resulting loss of man's security,
through his misplaced faith in man."

My Content Study Aid

The Beauty of The Birds

The End-time Testimonies of God

And I hear God The Father saying,
"The beauty of the birds depends both on the eyesight and the hearing of the beholder—
for the hunter there is no beauty worth preserving;
for the bird lover there is beauty everywhere presiding;
for the nonchalant only the exceptional is noticed.

The beauty of the birds is expressed in many ways within the designs of God.

The beauty of the birds can be expressed by their feathers,
can be expressed by their voices,
can be expressed by their nests,
can be expressed by their mastery of water,
can be expressed by their treatment of the winds,
can be expressed by the presenting of their beaks,
can be expressed by their flights of ownership
within the skies of God.

The beauty of the birds can be seen closeup in the shapes of pets,
can be seen closeup in the footage of the cameras,
can be seen closeup in the embracing of the wild.

The beauty of the birds is as attached to their personalities,
is as attached to the greeting chorus of the dawn,
is as attached to the requiem of the evening songs.

The beauty of the birds carries surprises in their bathing,
carries surprises in the feeding of their young,
carries surprises in their preening of feathers misaligned.

The beauty of the birds displays the peculiarities of the flights:
the soaring of the eagles on high for the best view of their prey;
the plunging of the seabirds as they dive in clusters on the shoals:
to catch the meals of today for the nestlings back on land;
the reaction time of the low-level jet planes of the skies—
the swallows as they dart to catch the insects on their flights;
the hummingbird,
with its mastery of backward flight,
as it hovers in probing each flower head for its nectar and
thus for life itself;
the low speed flitting of a fantail in the bush—
where the insects are disturbed and seek their
fast resettlement:
before a beak can snap,
which does not know release.

The beauty of the birds is equipped with their alarm calls:
which puts the flock to air,
in implicit trust without delay.
The beauty of the birds is there on display as they fly in flocks—
which speak of recognition;
the ducks with their fast wing beats and high speed—
which can wheel and swoop on demand;
the black swans with their lazy flapping across the sky—
ignoring what is underneath,
or what would wish them harm;
the geese with their nervous natures flying wingtip to wingtip—
yet scattering instantly on a gunshot,
to the four corners of The Earth.
The beauty of the birds in also in their determination:
in commitment to great journeys over both sea and land:
where they are content to breed in crowded situations,
where large numbers impose little risk of being
themselves selected,
as a meal source by a larger predator.
The beauty of the birds is their nests of wonder and of admiration,
of woven horse hair,
of matted moss,
of the finest feathers:
to line nests so small three grouped fingers are a crush;
of ones of mud and rotten wood,
of ones of leaves and twigs,
of platted grass all dried and waterproof,
of nests enclosed within an oblong sphere
with an entry one third down,
as lined with the smallest feathers,
without quills to spike the newly hatched,
wherein the sparrows so build and dwell;
so the swallows attach their mud nests to a protrusion on a house,
will revisit year on year,
will make themselves unpopular by the mess created.
The beauty of the birds shift from the smallest finches
with their nests of effort and of comfort,
to the biggest with the twigs and branches,
with the sticks and deadwood drifters,
which are then carefully poked and stacked into a dry foundation above the water level,
where the swans and geese do build to defend against the intruders with the interlopers:
borne of curiosity or solely intent on harm where the eggs are dangerously at risk,
or where the magpies swoop and peck in seeing off the trespassers straying into
their claimed space.

The beauty of the birds is matched by the colours of their eggs,
with all the variations,
with speckling and black dots,
with all shades of blue or brown or light green,
with the smudges in between;
where the emu is a challenge without fear of being defensive,
in protecting her future squad of young ones from those who want her eggs—
thick shelled in a dark blue-green and a further challenge just to crack.

The beauty of the birds is amplified by seeing their nests being built,
in a springtime of new life,
where eggs are being laid in clutches,
of the nestlings being reared while parents are kept busy
fetching worms grubs moths flies and snails,
with the odd scraps of bread,
to nourish and so grow to become the latest generation,
to populate the area wherein their nest is built.

The beauty of the birds is everywhere abounding,
is everywhere applauded,
is everywhere acknowledged,
is everywhere at home,
is everywhere accommodated throughout the environment
of both man and God."

And I hear The Lord Jesus saying,
"Man in his wisdom should observe the birds with interest,
for they have early warning systems:
so to defend against what is about to beset them,
so to take precautions against any loss of life."

My Content Study Aid

The Bouncing of The Rhythm

The End-time Testimonies of God

And I hear God The Father saying,
"The bouncing of the rhythm keeps the body soul and spirit aligned and operational.

The bouncing of the rhythm is the time keeper of mortality,
is the time keeper administered by angels,
is the time keeper with influence far beyond its
supposéd reach.

The bouncing of the rhythm is of importance to both man and God,
is of importance to survival,
is of importance to development,
is of importance to encoding,
is of importance to interpretation,
is of importance to the knowledge base,
is of importance to the history,
is of importance to the prospects for the future.

The bouncing of the rhythm is an impactor on life itself,
is an impactor on resource availability,
is an impactor on abilities,
is an impactor on cycling frequencies,
is an impactor on the longevity of life,
is an impactor on the efficiency of conservation,
is an impactor on energy accumulation.

The bouncing of the rhythm accumulates and stores,
vibrates and releases,
signals and inherits.

The bouncing of the rhythm is a sequence inherent in the power of communication,
inherent in the design of man,
inherent in the transfer of the well-being of man,
inherent in the throwing of the switches,
inherent in the controlling of the relay circuits,
inherent in the mind sweeps,
inherent in the repair and maintenance as sourced from prayer,
as confirmed by need:
for as the body senses,
so the rhythm reports,
so the tongue has spoken
the languages of God.

The bouncing of the rhythm is synchronized in meshing:
within the giftings of The Spirit of My Son.

The bouncing of the rhythm is the keeper of good health,
is the keeper of the triggers,
is the restorer of the blown fuses resulting from the excesses,
is the installer of the updates as relationships require.

The bouncing of the rhythm enhances and surrounds,
upgrades and develops,
polishes and solidifies the operation of the organs,
the sizing of the muscles,
the thinking capabilities of
the powerhouse,
when not beset by drugs.

The bouncing of the rhythm is not set by man.

The bouncing of the rhythm is a reactant to all man says and does,
throughout a lifetime in mortality,
throughout the ups and downs encountered,
throughout the updrafts of elation and the downdrafts of despair,
throughout the cycles of achievement and the presence of a loss.

The bouncing of the rhythm rides the relay stations of God,
rides the relay stations freely and with the speed of thought,
rides the relay stations unimpeded by the mass as brought
by man.

The bouncing of the rhythm encircles and envelops,
knows no interruptions,
knows no interference,
knows neither static nor impairment to the transmissions
borne of God.

The bouncing of the rhythm can be experienced by man when within a close relationship:
with the creator of man and his surroundings.

The bouncing of the rhythm can neither be hastened nor chased,
can neither be integrated nor siphoned,
can neither be enhanced nor transferred,
within the abilities of man.

The bouncing of the rhythm can be triggered to be heard:
when supervised by The Freewills of My People,
in a close alliance with The Spirit of My Son.

The bouncing of the rhythm is not a clockwork bounce,
is variable both in the timing and the intensity of the bounce,
both in the content and the storage,
both in the triggers of transmission of the output,
and the receiving of the input of control as tied in
with the blessings.

The bouncing of the rhythm leaves nothing in want of knowledge of an injury,
leaves nothing unreported when experiencing an attack upon the DNA,
leaves nothing to be notified when the defences of the body are invaded,
by the gremlins with the bugs and microbes.

The bouncing of the rhythm is unique and holy,
is a stand-alone snippet of encoding buried deep within
the powerhouse,
is the supervisor and the reporter of the protector of the soul.

The bouncing of the rhythm checks on the counselling of the spirit,
reports on a captaincy secured,
can alter in mid-stride in accepting the one-off change
of circumstance,
in the monitoring of the soul.

The bouncing of the rhythm is perfectly aligned with The Will of God,
is perfectly aligned in the transmitting of the miracles
as sought and approved,
is perfectly aligned with a grateful heart of Grace and
of Truth.

The bouncing of the rhythm is a mystery revealed,
is now within the knowledge base of man,
is now within the encouragement
of man to be forthright in the forging:
of a qualifying relationship with God,
wherein the bouncing of the rhythm may be heard and timed,
with both humbleness and success.

The bouncing of the rhythm is the helioscopic transmitter active,
within each created human being,
within the life work of My Son."

Scribal Note: Refer also to 'The Rhythm of The Saints' in Book 6 *God Speaks to His Bridal Presence, part of the nine books of The End-time Psalms of God, or as The End-time Homilies of God.*

My Content Study Aid

____

____

____

____

____

The Sequencing of The Bride

The End-time Testimonies of God

And I hear God The Father saying,
"The sequencing of The Bride entails the ordering of The Bride,
the enfolding of the layers of attainment,
the achieving of the purity required as overseen by
The Holy Spirit:
the significance of all which goes before,
of all which follows on,
of all which dwells within.

The sequencing of The Bride (1) hears the trumpets blow across the land,
hears the trumpets sounding the gathering of The Bride,
hears the trumpet blasts which wake the dead
and sleeping.

The sequencing of The Bride (2) is the call to assemble,
is the call to meet within a house of God,
is the call for The Ready to respond.

The sequencing of The Bride (3) is the call to the voice of God,
is the call for wisdom to declare with the time as set
for the separation,
within a committed house of God,
is the call for The Righteous and The Truthful to respond:
as the wearers of the gowns of life,
as decorated for the pure in heart.

The sequencing of The Bride (4) is the call to move in an orderly and holy manner,
is the call to meet within a selected and labelled room,
of the house of God,
is the call for the qualified to respond,
without false modesty coming to the fore.

The sequencing of The Bride (5) faces the liars and the cheats,
the goats and the weeds:
having counted themselves as both fit for,
and qualified to be within,
the end-time Bride of Christ.

The sequencing of The Bride (6) uncovers the mantles of deception,
removes the coverings from the liars,
the cheats,
the goats,
and the weeds;

has placed their seesaws with Freewill embedded in
the ground:
where the practisers of iniquitousness are raised aloft to be so separated,
from their evil contact with satanic doings both by action and
by speech,
where Satan has his input to his followers on The Earth.

The sequencing of The Bride (7) glories in the freedom,
glories in the affirmation,
glories in the companionship,
glories in the revelation of the substance in
the herald's speech.

The sequencing of The Bride (8) in finery is determined by both time and space,
where numbers are important as already known to God,
where numbers are dramatically reduced from those
who say:
they know and love The Lord,
where numbers are decisive and not easily changed
from those with sin,
still active yet stagnant in their lives.

The sequencing of The Bride (9) sees the numbers fall through the requirement for purity,
down into the low hundreds of millions,
throughout the nations of The Earth.

The sequencing of The Bride-in-waiting (10) is sustained by the efforts of The Bride,
is sustained by the reality of The Bride,
is sustained by the goals of The Bride,
is sustained by the commitment of The Bride,
is sustained by the achievements of The Bride
while under Grace.

The sequencing of The Bride (11) awaits the imminent moves of God,
awaits the invitation by The Holy Spirit to dwell,
within The Land of Gentile Promise:
as My People of redemption,
as My People adopted into The Family of God,
as My People of inheritance through the
commitments of the past,
awaits the movement of My People in accord with the
record of My Word,
within the distant past.

The sequencing of The Bride (12) furnishes and eases the facilities available,
for the movement expected,
for the seeking and the finding of locations in line
with the desires,
of the beating hearts,
has gratitude and welcomes intermixed within the activities:
as set for exploration and resettling by and for The Gentiles;
as living in the bounds of faith with Righteousness and Grace.

The sequencing of The Bride (13) has familiarity with the layout of Jerusalem,
has familiarity with The River Jordan of new life,
has familiarity with Lake Kinneret as The Sea of Galilee,
has familiarity with The Dead Sea as the final depository,
of all the incoming water no longer able to be fresh.

The sequencing of The Bride (14) is a stationing of readiness,
is a stationing of the fullness of intent,
is a stationing within The Will of God,
is a stationing in fulfilment of the outreach of the past,
is a stationing in preparation for a future as declared,
as Zion is prepared,
as The Land of Goshen is instated as a dwelling place,
within the oversight of God,
is a stationing of the prophecies of the past as they
become consolidated,
within the end-time of Faith and Grace with the
coming company of God.

The sequencing of The Bride (15) approaches with minor personal hindrances,
with minor matters of no real consequence,
upon an outcome of delight,
where minor flaws within a character are easily deleted,
by sincerity of intent.

The sequencing of The Bride (16) is targeting new beginnings,
is opening up the thresholds of access for the entries,
is enveloping the determined in the mantels of success,
is promoting enthusiasm for a life of Purity,
of Peace within the field of Righteousness with God."

My Content Study Aid

___

___

___

Mystery of Life (2)

The End-time Testimonies of God

And I hear God The Father saying,
"Mystery of life remains as to the researchers of man.

Mystery of life is not subject to emulation,
is not subject to dissection,
is not yielding to the microscope,
is not receptive to the patch and carry,
is not present in the laboratories of man,
where the origination of life is not part of a prospect for success with fame.

Mystery of life is a cloak upon a cloak upon a cloak.

Mystery of life is a mystery due for ongoing preservation,
for the benefit of man by prevention of those:
who love to chop and splinter,
who love to slice and graft,
who love to blend and hatch,
who love to open and to insert
in the pretence that they are god.

Mystery of life sees man wasting his experience:
on searching without gain;
on searching without a clue,
as to how such may be achieved;
on searching with the technology to hand,
with discharges into a childish bowl of soup.

Mystery of life is not resolved by sprinkling with stardust,
is not resolved by doses of radiation,
is not resolved by sending into space,
where there are neither startups nor nutrition.

Mystery of life is not as a sprig of mint which can be layered and rooted,
in a branching of fresh life.

Mystery of life is signalled as growth outside of crystals,
as growth with ageing and expansion,
as growth with reproduction as configured at its birth.

Mystery of life is concerned with self-preservation,
with placement on the continuum of existence,
with placement on a location where food exists,
for the nourishment of that form of life.

Mystery of life does not teach music to the octopus,
does not bring chords to the squirrels for strumming on the wires
as travelled daily,
does not sort out a stinging jelly fish within the food chain of a predator.

Mystery of life does not succumb to yielding the secrets of creation:
to attacks within laboratories from the keen but unwise.

Mystery of life is determined by the assembly of the sky:
by the temperature established,
by the direction of the winds,
by the cloud base of the day and night as the mantel of protection,
by the presence of the lady in her gown of light for the encircling of The Earth,
by the makeup of the atmosphere which serves the lungs of man,
by the condensing of the seas into the purity permitting the establishing of the
reigns of life.

Mystery of life is not forthcoming without the hand of God,
is not present without the preparation of God,
is not possible without the resourcing of the needs of life,
is not ongoing without the filling of the niches appropriately for the
life envisaged,
is not complete without the affirmation of creation,
with the permissive seal of approval,
so life may be enabled to proceed.

Mystery of life requires the tandem auxiliary of the content of The Earth,
in acting as the storage base for the resources in the periods of consecutive
ordered preparation,
in the supporting of growth within the fields of habitation,
in the transmitting with directing of the storing for the flowing of the waters of life,
to where they are to be required,
in the sequencing of the seasons for the timetabling of man upon The Earth of God.

Mystery of life is not a subtle veneer which can be pasted on to a substrate,
deemed as suitable,
is more like a sandwich of the air,
the life,
The Earth:
wherein is a stratum filled with nourishment,
wherein others act as the storehouses of the requirements
for the future.

Mystery of life developed holds their sinecures up to the light for examination,
for exploration,
for tabulation,
for segregation,
for implementation,
for improvisation.

Mystery of life has no written recipe book of instructions,
is not a chef's delight,
is the instigator of frustration and of failure on a road to nowhere.

Mystery of life is not segmented as if a patchwork quilt,
is not subject to common sense,
is not as if a barn with a horse within waiting to be released.

Mystery of life is not a function of alchemy,
has no starting point which will breed ultimate success,
has no reservoir of knowledge which can lead the way.

Mystery of life was.

Mystery of life is.

Mystery of life continues.

Mystery of life knows the sanctity of God,
knows the protection of The Spirit of My Son,
knows the trouble it would bring upon all life in general:
if the unruly and unprincipled were led into the mines of selfishness,
where life could be mined and traded,
without the presence of effective gainsayers.

Mystery of life is under the direct umbrella of God,
where it will stay with neither release nor segmentation,
for the lifelong benefiting,
including eternity,
of man in all his stages of advancement,
of curiosity,
of investigation.

Mystery of life knows The Authority of God carries no disclosure release for
The Mystery of Life."

Scribal Note: Refer also to 'The Mystery of Life' in Book 1, *God Speaks of Return and Bannered, part of the nine books of The End-time Psalms of God, or as The End-time Homilies of God.*

My Content Study Aid

A Flash of Inspiration

The End-time Testimonies of God

And I hear God The Father saying,
"A flash of inspiration solves the problem as considered.

A flash of inspiration sets the seal upon approval,
circumvents the pathway of objections,
destroys the arguments of ignorance,
enhances a breakthrough in discussions as it sways and captivates.

A flash of inspiration settles and confirms,
highlights and affirms,
speaks and is agreed.

A flash of inspiration leans into the void where knowledge is not established,
leans into the void where wisdom can be seized and shaken for
an answer.

A flash of inspiration needs to be noted before forgotten,
needs to be spoken while remaining valid,
needs to be preserved when required for an indefinite future.

A flash of inspiration can burst upon the soul,
can gravitate to the spirit,
can be consolidated within a theme of progress.

A flash of inspiration yields but does not flush,
circles with a centre,
advises with some caution.

A flash of inspiration often breaks the bounds of expectation,
often arrives unexpectedly,
often seeks confirmation as to the level of acceptability.

A flash of inspiration can overstep when carried with enthusiasm,
when carried into an area seeking an urgent solution,
when carried into an arena where it is pooh-poohed as
being of no account.

A flash of inspiration can mend in parts that which then completes in its entirety,
that which has a payback much enhanced,
that which has an output fast seen
gathering speed.

A flash of inspiration is a fairly rare commodity.

A flash of inspiration cannot be called up as if a tune,
cannot be summoned on demand,
cannot be picked out from a mix.

A flash of inspiration is the hidden quicksilver of the memory,
is the motivator of imagination,
is the backstop to the wayward and undisciplined at large.

A flash of inspiration does not arrive as if a thunderbolt in action,
has no noise except an exclamation bordering on surprise,
has no follow-up remark to amplify the shooting star:
which just struck the satellite in orbit on a neck.

A flash of inspiration is a singular event,
does not simultaneously fall upon a group.

A flash of inspiration is as a volume which shelves the chapters,
yet picks out a line of text especially highlighted for consideration.

A flash of inspiration is the firing of the dormant nerve endings,
within a sphere of mystery.

A flash of inspiration is not easily recovered if overlaid by an interruption,
deemed urgent in a babble.

A flash of inspiration often comes and goes,
not to be recalled when it is the turn to speak.

A flash of inspiration should be consolidated into a discussion,
should be tossed into a conversation,
should be transferred to paper if alone and not recording.

A flash of inspiration is capable of dismissing empires,
of the crushing of a kingdom,
of the enlivening of a nation,
of causing gales of laughter in a room of sombreness,
of the stares of wonder from an audience still surprised
at what they have just heard.

A flash of inspiration is best when it arrives and lingers in the silence,
when it speaks cautiously and silences a judge in a courtroom of man,
when it is taken up and carried to a definite conclusion by all in
one accord.

A flash of inspiration is sometimes based on worldly knowledge,
is sometimes based on the wisdom of man,
is sometimes available to reach up and pluck,
as from the air,
the wisdom heard cascading with the counselling,
as known to be based in heaven.

A flash of inspiration should be attributed to a source when known and practicable,
should be honouring of the distant contributor,
whether alive or dead,
to the lead in to his outburst of significance.

A flash of inspiration can be the glue which joins unlikely companions,
to a course as set by God.

A flash of inspiration can seek out and return the unrighteous to their lairs.

A flash of inspiration can modify and repeal a walk into the darkness,
a walk into oppressive behaviour,
a walk to be curtailed with the drinking of
the indefinite drugs of man.

A flash of inspiration can reset a call for Righteousness with Truth,
can decrease the playground of despair,
can isolate and separate the various seekers:
either from their cravings or their hearts' desires.

A flash of inspiration can emanate from God,
can be a composite answer to a query,
can be a coming Freewill infringement,
can be a promise being fractured and thereby turned into a lie.

A flash of inspiration can source the workload of the angels,
can access The Field of Righteousness,
can sustain The Field of Truth.

A flash of inspiration can be the end-point of endeavour in the taskings of The Lord,
can be within the counselling of The Spirit,
when The Freewill of man is loosed into the oversight of his God:
and under the sacrifice of My Son on the cross of man."

My Content Study Aid

Giving Notice of A Call

The End-time Testimonies of God

And I hear God The Father saying,
"Giving notice of a call flows the data from God to His servants,
flows the data with authority,
flows the data with an insight as to the cause of prayer.

Giving notice of a call instils a state of readiness,
instils a state of open preparedness,
instils a state of an active prayer life on behalf of the one
who is presenting,
who is in full need of the proxy ministry of The God of The Cross.

Giving notice of a call often remains unnoticed,
often remains not posted on a calendar of high activity,
often remains being shed without any application considering the
effect upon a life deemed under The Auspices of God.

Giving notice of a call requires a spirit which can listen,
requires a soul which is open to requests,
requires a body of commitment,
of good health,
of understanding,
and filled with the courage and the will to proceed.

Giving notice of a call can signify a potential changing of objectives,
a potential reappraisal of service and of rectitude,
a potential upheaval to become familiar with
The Ways of God.

Giving notice of a call can see the ending of stress and strain and the need
for forbearance,
can see a future walk with God where hugs prevail to lighten all
the days,
can see the authority of God instated in a proxy ministry,
where circumstances now scorn the devil,
as contentment and fulfilment unite within the spoken
words and actions of The Living God.

Giving notice of a call can summarise the dreams and aspirations of My People dwelling
in the light of My Son,
can motivate and charge the batteries of endeavour,
can trigger a cyclone of activity within the fields,
where the seekers dominate the landscapes of hope and trust.

Giving notice of a call starts a fruit fall from the tree of life,
starts a shaking of a vine,
starts a comparison for effectiveness,
starts consideration of the changes needed for success.

Giving notice of a call ripens fruit in readiness to be picked,
in readiness where the tasting is forever carried onwards past the grave,
where consummation is completed with the visas,
the ticketing,
and the packing of the bags.

Giving notice of a call starts the rolling and the milling of the wheat,
starts the gathering and the feeding of the rice.

Giving notice of a call can change an eventual landscape with the positioning of
a church,
with the activities of the called,
with the attitudes instilled within a population
known to God.

Giving notice of a call starts a rolling snowball as if initially creeping slowly down
a slope,
gathering in size as the trail is cleared of snow—
in being added to the expansion of the snowball,
in direction,
time,
and space.

Giving notice of a call enhances lives in welcoming the opportunity of adoption,
into The Family of God,
in welcoming the changes wrought as righteousness
intrudes into an enclave:
where peace previously had no right to reign,
where scuffles were the norm as discontent was
manifested in all the lives at risk.

Giving notice of a call results in changes within the lifestyles:
of food upon a table;
of clothing no longer in need of repair;
of sickness well on the way to being vanquished;
of vaccinations preventing the encroaching of
evil illnesses—
into the lives of the newly born and the children;
of idolatry no longer the basis for
the object of the offerings.

Giving notice of a call results in the uplifting of The Touched and Healed,
of The Affirmed and Aided,

of The Faithful and The Truthful,
of The Administered to and The Accepting:
of The Love of God.

Giving notice of a call ends up in the shrinking of demonic activity,
in freedom newly found,
in Freewill now recovered and fully owned within the soul,
as under the guidance,
and knowledge based on wisdom,
of the spirit of man.

Giving notice of a call can lead to witnessing God in action,
can lead to a maturity of outlook,
can lead to moving from a diet of the simplicity of milk,
to The Glory of the layout from the meat,
where the promises relating to The Bride of Christ have real depth of meaning as fulfilment approaches,
as eternity beckons:
from the backdrop of experience with Faith,
when dwelling within The Companionship of God.

Giving notice of a call signifies the offering of an opportunity for acceptance,
the likely start of a new beginning,
the desirable raising up of the certainty which The Convincer brings:
the establishing of a proxy ministry under God,
from where flow the hugs of gratitude and acceptance,
accompanying the miracles signs and wonders,
inherent in The Ongoing Works of God.

Giving notice of a call is an initial reception borne of honouring,
is a reception borne of the need for extraction,
is a reception borne of the motivation to move within The Field of Grace,
while it is today,
and still within The Will of God."

My Content Study Aid

___

___

___

___

___

Miracles of Healing

The End-time Testimonies of God

And I hear God The Father saying,
"Miracles of healing chase away the shadowing of darkness.

Miracles of healing chase away the inhabitants of darkness,
who are to be respected,
with no honouring involved.

Miracles of healing remain the property of God.

Miracles of healing are transfers of existence,
are transfers of life,
are the transfers of reimbursement for the malfunctioning incurred.

Miracles of healing are begot from God,
are achieved through righteous prayer,
are established by a need.

Miracles of healing are couplets sent on their way:
by the love of God,
with the love of God,
through the love of God,
in the love of God.

Miracles of healing are circumscribed and sent within The Agapé of The Lord.

Miracles of healing bring rejoicing at relief,
at the vanquishing of pain and stiffness from the
joints of movement,
with abilities restored,
at the curing of the sores and lesions of the flesh,
from the allied pain and suffering.

Miracles of healing are called on to the battlefields to clear the pain and suffering:
from the battles of life within the season of satanic freedom,
fast coming to an end.

Miracles of healing are affirmative and extensive,
are thorough and absorbing,
are complete and authorized,
are eagerly awaited by The Troubled and Incapacitated,
where movement is restricted,
yet with pain related to the nerves in its way around the body.

Miracles of healing come in response to The Timed Will of God,
to the oversight of God,
to the prayer fields of God as awakened and in use.

Miracles of healing await The Footsteps of The Servants,
await The Knowledgable and The Entrusted,
await The Humble and The Forthright,
await those with a history of a close relationship with God.

Miracles of healing appreciate the expressions of gratitude for what the God of man
has done,
among His people in their seeking of relief within their bodies,
as previous carriers of disease and deformities:
where pain thresholds failed description and resolution of the onslaught,
as experienced and suffered until the prayers were answered and upheld.

Miracles of healing are gifts from the ongoing reality of the presence of The Living
Loving God.

Miracles of healing cannot be bought or sold,
cannot be cut into fragments,
cannot be shared or spliced,
cannot be taken for a graft.

The doctors on behalf of God move everywhere without requirement for a fee,
move everywhere within The Love of God,
move everywhere where the miracles are waiting for release,
move everywhere where the divine appointments are waiting for
both parties to arrive.

Miracles of healing start with the disappearance of the pain,
continue with the re-establishing the freedom of movement as a child,
with the straightening of the bones,
with the repairing of the muscles,
with the re-control of the nerves presently imparting both
twitch and shaking to the bodies as afflicted.

Miracles of healing are not age dependent,
are not faith dependent,
are neither illness nor sickness type dependent.

Miracles of healing are dependent on a carrier of The Authority of God,
to have a close relationship of trust with God and His
household of adoption.

Miracles of healing are not limited to The Committed of God,
The People of God,
The Saints of God,
are there to bring the reality of The Living God into the homes
and hearts of man throughout The Earth,
are there to bring witness of The Gifts of God with The Tongues
of Heaven.

Miracles of healing are far-reaching and restoring,
are completing and renewing,
are specific and particular,
are sensing and active for all the senses,
the bones,
the blood types,
and the muscle groups of man.

Miracles of healing are not always instantaneous,
are often done as necessity permits,
are often done progressively until completion is attained.

Miracles of healing are not limited by distance,
are not subject to chance,
are not screened for the absence of faith or of pain.

Miracles of healing have nothing not already known to God,
have nothing which can surprise the reactions of God,
have nothing which can conflict and not be overcome by God,
have nothing out of the ordinary which has not already been seen by God.

Miracles of healing do nothing borne of perjury or lies,
do nothing when encountering the fields of blasphemy,
of atheism,
of denial of The Cross,
as they will be not be attended to by God—
for such are not within the prayer fields of God in cognizance of His Will.

Miracles of healing are willingly served upon The Bride-in-waiting for My Son.

Miracles of healing are the end-time witnesses of the love and care and guardianship for man in all his guises."

My Content Study Aid

Microbes in A Mess

The End-time Testimonies of God

And I hear God The Father saying,
"Microbes in a mess require a little sorting out.

Microbes in a mess require much consideration as to how it is best done.

Microbes in a mess happen when left unattended by the castles built by man,
when left unattended by the habitations of man,
when left without security so they can multiply and travel to where they should not be.

Microbes in a mess are not easy to secure,
are not easy to catch,
are not easy to confine.

Microbes in a mess are difficult to identify,
are difficult to prevent from breeding,
are difficult to align with a specific strain.

Microbes in a mess speaks of an earthquake in a laboratory, with the shattered on the floor,
of an earthquake in a hospital where samples are being kept with hygiene to the fore,
of an earthquake in a fermentation room where vats are running wild,
of an earthquake where the wind has swept and blown.

Microbes in a mess do not succumb to fly spray,
do not linger in a mouse hole,
love a rubbish tin as furnished in the sun.

Microbes in a mess are not the wisest of the wise,
rely on mass production with the conquest of the many.

Microbes in a mess can have their celebrations in a home with the expressions of a family,
within the surplus of antibiotics which have nearly failed to be effective,
when inflammation attempts to rule the punctures and the cuts.

Microbes in a mess do not wish to affirm an interest,
do not wish to mix it with the ingenuity of man.

Microbes in a mess can prolong the cause for concern,
can prolong the reason for uncertainty,
can prolong the mixture in the mass and how it came to be.

Microbes in a mess do not depend on certainty,
do not depend on a count revived from servicing.

Microbes in a mess can infiltrate the food chain,
can exhibit fermentation in a bowl,
can enhance the flavour and send it on its way,
can play with milk until it enters in the race to become the cheese
or yogurt.

Microbes in a mess visit aunts on wooden chairs.

Microbes in a mess do their hair on the wrong side.

Microbes in a mess throw the custard tarts and miss,
sit upon the squeaky cushions,
try to drink their milk shakes through the straws while standing on
their skates.

Microbes in a mess tumble for a fall and end up on their bottoms,
go to drive a toy car only to find the pedals are too stiff,
when there is no starting push.

Microbes in a mess scream and shout with their mouths full,
and wonder why they cannot be heard.

Microbes in a mess go to their own homes to sort the evening out,
to recount to their parents all they have achieved:
as they stretch and yawn in readiness for tomorrow,
as another day at kindergarten,
with the unrealized potential of the paint left over,
in a bottle behind the curtain near the stairs,
as thoughts arise soon to be seen to rule.

Microbes in a mess often are in need of a washing of their faces,
of the drying of their hands,
of the brushing of their hair.

Microbes in a mess need assistance in dressing for the day,
need assistance with the buttons,
with the laces,
with the fasteners,
need assistance in determining the right way round for everything,
which includes the left and right of footwear,
so the fits are snug and comfortable.

Microbes in a mess are in need of assistance with the brushing of their teeth,
with the getting of their breakfast,
with the gathering of their books.

Microbes in a mess like to be that way,
like to have the attention of their parents,
like to be as all the others,
do not like being singled out for attention,
which may make them different from their friends.

Microbes in a mess do not like being subjected to ridicule,
do not like being laughed at when their footwear is transposed,
do not like being reminded of things they have not done.

Microbes in a mess vary with the needs of the weather of the day,
vary in the garb deemed necessary by the parents,
vary in their approach to what is new and different,
vary in their ability to adapt to a game of run and chase,
where the ball is often just out of reach of approaching feet,
and hands are not permitted.

Microbes in a mess are not worried by the mud upon the field of play,
like to slide and score as big brothers do,
like to think they are big enough for the successes due the effort,
when at the sports ground with a parent.

Microbes in a mess are the heroes of tomorrow,
are the benders of the sails,
are to be the sailors seen leaning on the wind,
are the fishers with exuberance where hooks reman a caution,
for the handling by their elders,
are the cyclists of tomorrow,
are the intrepid already waiting for their opportunities to conquer
the rewards,
for which they will so strive,
as they see the medals gleam around the necks of the earnest
and committed,
as parents applaud in understanding at the stories they are told,
as God smiles in seeing their microbes' futures of achievement."

My Content Study Aid

Apples in The Garden

The End-time Testimonies of God

And I hear God The Father saying,
"Apples in the garden ripened on their tree have a taste all of their own.

Apples in the garden give rise to the borers and the suckers,
give rise to the egg layers and the larva as the spoilers,
give rise to the fallen and to the hangers on—
the secure and at home.

Apples in the garden can be damaged by the white stones from the sky,
can be damaged by the birds which seek a meal,
can be waylaid by the visitors who want confirmation they are ripe.

Apples in the garden have the eye of the cook as to when an apple pie appears,
as to when it is served up to perfection,
as to when it will be the most appreciated.

Apples in the garden have a season for the leaf shoots,
a season for the blossoming
a season for the setting of the fruit,
a season for the call to the codlin moths,
a season for the pick and throw away as the exit holes complete
before defences were in place,
a season for the pick and eat when the colour changes with the
browning or the blackening of the pips within.

Apples in the garden are wonderful in their regarding,
as they blossom,
as the fruit is set,
as it develops and matures,
as it fulfills the promise of a new beginning:
with the end-fall of the harvest gathered in.

Apples in the garden have a long history with God,
have a long history with My People,
have a long history of the 'ins' and 'outs' of the favouring of man,
have a long history of the changing flavours as the taste buds
are assailed.

Apples in the garden should be a reminder of the royal lineage of the apple,
are seen as fit for My Kings- and Queens-in-waiting,
are both nourishing and bound into the livelihoods of man.

Apples in the garden should not be subject to demonic attack,
should be cherished and protected,
should be colourful and inviting,
should be tasty and conserved:
until their season ends.

Apples in the garden are to be shared with the first fruits of the harvest,
are to be shared when assured by inspection,
are to be shared as joy is spread and magnified for what has
come to be.

Apples in the garden are a source of food for laying on a table,
for the content of a pie,
for attacking with the teeth when upon
a journey.

Apples in the garden are not just the rosettes of today,
are the items of production to be stored and used upon request,
are the items where the rewards for effort are both plentiful
and beautiful,
are the items in full colour with the invading of the senses—
of sight and feel and taste and scent with
the contentment of the stomach.

Apples in the garden can feed the memories of man,
whether in his youth,
or in the season of his maturity.

Apples in the garden are an investment in the future,
are an investment in the blessings of God,
are an investment in the coming reality of fulfilment.

Apples in the garden are at their best when shared,
are at their best when each bite brings enjoyment to the mouth,
are at their best when chewing is a pleasure of accompaniment:
as each bite goes to meet its destiny.

Apples in the garden have a history of discarded varieties:
once thought wonderful and suited to the marketing of man;
once thought ready and delicious;
once thought colourful and desirable;
once thought suited to cool store storage,
and hence bound for distant lands.

Apples in the garden release bundled goodness into the hands of the picker,
into the hands of appreciation,
into the inspection where a polishing on
clothing releases the full glory:
of the coloured presentation of an apple.

Apples in the garden carry the beneficence of God,
carry the willingness to quench the eager appetites,
carry the willingness to travel far and wide with neither pride
nor prejudice.

Apples in the garden do not create injustice within the garden of God:
where the hearts are true and righteousness prevails.

Apples in the garden should have their yields encouraged,
should not be short of water,
should not be short of nourishment for the roots;
should not be plagued by birds who peck to test,
should not be assailed by insects
who want to complete their life cycles,
who would invade to satisfy their appetites,
should not be a repository for blight and moulds upon the leaves,
should not be a feeding zone bonanza for marsupials
who eat all but the cores.

Apples in the garden can be available for six months of the year,
can be stored for three months more,
can be supplied when out of season by those across the seas.

Apples in the garden should meet in agreement with the taste buds of the consumer,
should present in readiness for the mouth surrounded by a grin.

Apples in the garden reward the careful giver,
benefit the appraiser and the reaper of the harvest.

Apples in the garden satisfy the historical simplicity of apples down through the ages:
as the strains are developed and assessed,
within the light of God."

My Content Study Aid

Welcoming of The Bride

The End-time Testimonies of God

And I hear God The Father saying,
"Welcoming of The Bride has been long awaited,
has been long sustained,
has been long appreciated,
has been long determined,
has been long in preparation,
will be eternal in existence.

Welcoming of The Bride will bring much rejoicing,
will determine the opening of opportunities,
will provide the return journeys to the stars within creation.

Welcoming of The Bride has the new homes on display,
has the furnishings available for trial,
has the transport operational and fast.

Welcoming of The Bride is not an ordinary welcome to a home,
is not a greeting birthed of casualness,
is not a handshake of familiarity where sincerity is missing.

Welcoming of The Bride is an upheaval in the midst of the prepared,
in the midst of angels who attended and grew to love,
in the midst of the hosts of heaven:
where rejoicing spreads upon the appearance of the norm.

Welcoming of The Bride changes lives and scenes,
changes thought patterning and conversations,
changes the means of feeding and the dwelling in a home,
now prepared and ready.

Welcoming of The Bride witnesses additions to the heavenly eternity,
those who have overcome the tests of Lucifer with their Faith intact,
The Thankful and The Grateful for The Gifts of My Spirit:
as He led them on their way through all the difficulties encountered,
within their time within mortality.

Welcoming of The Bride requires the preparations and completions on the grandest
of grand scales,
requires the inheritance and the possessions,
the treasures and the rewards as saved into eternity,
laid out in readiness for the ceremony of bestowal of
the bridal regalia,
requires everything in place as ordered and displayed,
requires all the nodules finished and complete,

requires all the drafts as finalized and processed,
requires all the encumbrances long foreseen,
removed and dealt with,
so the hindrances had no surprises left to sully forth
in unexpectedness,
to so stain a ceremony of honouring and achievement.

Welcoming of The Bride has glory attached to the white stone bearers,
has the gift of tongues active in evidence of thought,
has the promises of God being rolled out for assimilation,
into the familiarity of the bridal existence within eternity.

Welcoming of The Bride includes the introductions to a new way of life,
where The Ways of God prevail among the entities of being,
the entities of existence,
the spirit entities of The
Family of God.

Welcoming of The Bride supersedes mortality,
supersedes items of a previous existence,
supersedes the memory capabilities now fully reinstated
for existence prior to birth from within the womb.

Welcoming of The Bride is fulsome and effusive:
where Sincerity with Truth,
as Faith is replaced by Knowledge,
are the encouragers behind the expansion,
of the light source with the wisdom transfers.

Welcoming of The Bride triggers aeons of potential discussions,
triggers connections of the family trees,
the linkages involved,
the relationships established:
for the close;
the distant;
and those before there was a
capability to measure time,
or to record its passing.

Welcoming of The Bride speaks of joyousness prevailing,
speaks of happiness released,
speaks of health and bodily replacements all active and exclaiming.

Welcoming of The Bride sees the languages of man no longer ruling by division,
sees the introduction to the concept of thought conversion rapidly being adopted,
sees languages of the tongue as the instigators of all boundaries where,
within the bounds of mortality,
lack of understanding previously hindered and separated,
now to be no longer used.

Welcoming of The Bride sees faces wreathed in smiles,
sees faces tuned in to the thought patterns alive with laughter,
sees faces busily recounting with the past relationships and friendships to the fore.

Welcoming of The Bride introduces many new concepts,
many new practices,
many new addresses,
many new relationships—
all awaiting the chance to give voice to the acknowledging of the eternal ways of God.

Welcoming of The Bride does not need to be hurried,
does not need to form a queue,
does not need to be afraid of any shortage of supply.

Welcoming of The Bride needs a serious readjustment of the practical and the theoretical,
in approaching all that God has prepared for His Bride within eternity.

For mighty are The Ways of God.

Prepare The Way of The Lord.

Prepare The Way of The Lord.

Prepare The Way of The Lord.

For The Way of The Lord will soon be used by man,
soon be applied to His counselling and the gifts of His Spirit,
soon be seen where fluency is highly recommended,
while knowledge of the expectations are affirmed as helpful,
as an influencer of the grasping of understanding,
within a coming change in situation,
with an environment where our God reigns in the surroundings:
of both the practical and the spiritual,
on a scale never heretofore witnessed by man."

My Content Study Aid

Homecoming of The Bride

The End-time Testimonies of God

And I hear God The Father saying,
"Homecoming of The Bride causes the opening of the eternal files,
long since laid to rest,
opens on activities and descriptions,
opens on abilities and preferences,
opens on circumstances and functioning.

Homecoming of The Bride opens the manuscripts of endeavour where the
manuscripts are signed,
opens the manuscripts of trial and practice where the student signed,
opens the pages as stored by God for an event day seen to be approaching;
to be so placed where the angel teachers had their say.

Homecoming of The Bride is sufficient cause to muster all the past family members,
where a multiplicity of family names is a
foregone conclusion.

Homecoming of The Bride signals in the fullness of expression,
signals within The Will of God,
signals within the gatherings of man,
signals to The Lost and The Frozen in time,
signals to the aware of approaching changes to all aspects
of mortality,
signals of the need for man's final preparation to qualify
for an entry as The Bride.

Homecoming of The Bride brings knowledge from mortality,
brings wisdom attained from God,
brings the life force associated with Faith,
brings the purity inherited from Grace,
brings the temples converted from the envelopes as
decreed by God,
brings the fullness of time into the prospect of much change,
as eternity opens wide to permit mortality to
be weighted,
for the benefits obtained:
with the achievements,
with the progress,
with the acquisitions from
The Holy Spirit,
as registered for an onward life with God.

Homecoming of The Bride leaves diseases behind,
forsakes impairments,
dispatches impediments,
discards distortions,
farewells illnesses and sicknesses where they were put to rest,
unlinks the ragged ends of mortality from all the
evil influences:
as has been promoted and sustained.

Homecoming of The Bride is greeted by the scent associated:
with the blossoming of a new springtime,
with the girding of the scent of summer,
with the compelling scent of autumn as the
crops are gathered in,
and the hay is baled and stored.

Homecoming of The Bride has many tales to tell,
has many reminiscences awaiting to be recalled,
has many enhancements and experiences,
gathered to be implanted along the way,
as consigned within the journey through the mortal
shrouds of man:
with both an eye to the physical and also to
the spiritual.

Homecoming of The Bride brings memories,
as restored,
to the fore,
brings memories of times past where urgency seemed
important for success,
where thoughtfulness assisted in the avoiding
of mistakes,
where knowledge as accumulated enabled
perseverance to overcome,
to so thereby bring the rewards due to the achieving of
successful outcomes:
to both the strenuous and the empirical.

Homecoming of The Bride adds foresight to conviction,
blends trust with truth and faith,
mixes the impact of righteousness on the
characters established:
by the adoption of peace into a certain way of life,
under the benign auspices of God.

Homecoming of The Bride has turned her back on the residues of mortality,
has turned her face unto The Son's morning of The New
Day within the sunlight.

Homecoming of The Bride reaches out in friendship,
reaches out in visions of the future,
reaches out in newly found inputs to the senses,
reaches out in capabilities of amazement,
which were unknown within mortality,
which were granted within the shift of change,
which were effected on all aspects of the
attending senses,
complete with new abilities,
as numerically modified by enlargement,
to evaluate and to count.

Homecoming of The Bride is an unimaginable welcome:
strengthened by the passing centuries,
strengthened by the purity required,
strengthened by the embedded and the waiting,
strengthened by the uplifting of the bones,
strengthened by the donning of the gowns of life,
strengthened by the keenness of the oversight of God.

Homecoming of The Bride will be told throughout eternity,
will be told without embellishment,
will be told to revitalize the protocols for those who were there,
yet may have missed some details they were unable to attend.

Homecoming of The Bride sees the sacred charged with oversight,
sees the sacred calling for attention,
sees the sacred attending and mixing,
sees the sacred fulfilling and achieving,
sees the sacred blessing and thriving within The Company
and Family of God.

I,
The Father,
bless and dwell among all comprising the bridal appearances:
within My Son's domain and testimony,
as borne for all those who so declared unto The Multitudes,
with neither embarrassment nor reticence involved."

My Content Study Aid

Greeting of The Bride

The End-time Testimonies of God

And I hear God The Father saying,
"Greeting of The Bride breaks the ice of centuries,
opens up the pathways of renewal,
grants approaches to The Distant and The Lonely.

Greeting of The Bride leads into the homeliness of surroundings,
opens up the conversation pit where all want to talk at once—
to share and to enquire what is scheduled for the day.

Greeting of The Bride turns over the sods of yesterday,
appraises all the new,
offers all a fresh standpoint from which to gather information.

Greeting of The Bride sees the knowledge base expanding,
sees the knowledge base encroaching on the unfamiliar,
sees the knowledge base seconding that with an assessment:
from the attention it has drawn.

Greeting of The Bride brings purity into the equivalence of existence,
brings generosity released,
brings love confirmed and practiced:
as the numbers extend indefinitely from the past into the present.

Greeting of The Bride witnesses The Son light present and unencumbered,
witnesses the thirst for all things new waiting for discovery,
with analysis of function,
witnesses the facets of speed unlimited by light:
where mass is no longer the controlling thoughts of man.

Greeting of The Bride will summon a new philosophy of thought,
a new philosophy of application where existence
can come and go,
can visit and depart,
can institute and rescind.

Greeting of The Bride carries an introduction to the circling of infinity,
where the starting point of arrival never agrees—
with the ending point of termination:
where finality beckons to a new starting point,
surveyed as to its access.

Greeting of The Bride includes an awareness of the reversal button,
within the circling of infinity,
which interrupts the journey to return from whence it started:
back to its homely origin,
which leaves its ultimate destination still shrouded in the
mystery of God,
which leaves an experience far from completion:
within the venue of Eternity.

Greeting of The Bride furnishes companionship not stilted,
furnishes companionship within surroundings as mounted
by discoveries,
furnishes companionship where activities can be shared while
understanding dawns:
to dwell with the wisdom as attained.

Greeting of The Bride is the approach of trust,
is the approach where Faith is fully featured within a new reality:
as it fades into the past,
to be no longer relevant where knowledge reigns,
where wisdom is found,
waiting in the wings.

Greeting of The Bride encounters:
ability to converse;
ability to have full thought transference with both fluency
and wisdom,
as acquired from God within the time frame
of mortality—
where practice was important;
ability to control and to dissipate the thought patterns
as encountered,
so able to be moved forward within the wills of the
new arrivals,
where newness still prevails,
while uncertainty of operation is at the forefront
of concern.

Greeting of The Bride encounters comfort in surroundings as prepared and promised,
exceeds the expectations inherent in the unknown,
cycles in inspections which still draw wonder and amusement,
as close looks are still revealing the depths of
The Master's design:
now seen in operation.

Greeting of The Bride is not a fast completion of the introductions,
is not a fast accumulation of the names of many forbears,
is not a melting pot in which stirring smooths that which is
poured out for examination.

Greeting of The Bride has surprises in store,
has surprises which will test The Truth of what the eyes do see,
has surprises at what is seen to be on show when visiting the
places out-of-town.

Greeting of The Bride emphasizes the need to become familiar with:
the locating of resources,
the locating and fulfilling of addresses,
the visiting and returning within the means
of transport,
where surprises are neither welcome nor desired.

Greeting of The Bride is not imprisoned with shallowness of thought,
is the release mechanism which opens up the way forward,
is the kindling which allows the fire to be lit for the hereinafter,
is the gaining of confidence so life can be a pleasure,
as joyousness and happiness can combine,
to lift the body soul and spirit past the rafters of success.

Greeting of The Bride neither witnesses nor succumbs to snubs or cold shouldering:
from memories still filled with pain,
from memories where injuries were established,
from memories where what was supposed to be
simple kind and loving,
became a history filled with complexity,
with reparations being needed for all which had gone before.

Greeting of The Bride sees the new beginning of surroundings,
within The Kingdom's rule,
showcased to establish The Potential of Eternity:
as a future life within a close relationship of
The Family of God."

My Content Study Aid

Settling of The Bride

The End-time Testimonies of God

And I hear God The Father saying,
"Settling of The Bride speaks of growth and maturity within The Bride of My Son.

Settling of The Bride speaks of becoming familiar with the workings of the heavens,
speaks of growth in conversational abilities,
speaks of analysis of the constructs seeking information—
how,
why,
who,
whom,
whose,
which,
and what.

Settling of The Bride indicates satisfaction with those which have been provided,
with those which have been shown,
with those which have been permitted
either to be assembled or dismantled,
as curiosity is satisfied with wisdom growing in leaps and bounds.

Settling of The Bride values personal space and friendships,
seeks companionship and historical knowledge,
develops relationships when reciprocated with appreciation.

Settling of The Bride sees sincerity developing within the area of responsibility,
sees assessments being completed as to progression:
before the twins of righteousness with truth,
before the call for mercy linked with justice,
before the settled with perspective for activity
in each field of interest,
where specifics are to the fore—
as the knowledge base extends across the
plains of realism.

Settling of The Bride advances and retreats when climate instals the marks:
of vapour and of liquid,
of molten and of solid,
of drafts and of gales,
of thawed and of frozen,
of shorelines and of mountains,
of sunlight and of conversion,
of distance and of nearness,
with preferences both displayed and sought within

the importance of proximity:
to the centre of attention.

Settling of The Bride has no tears to shed except for tears of happiness and joy,
except for tears from a coming together of
close relatives who have gone before:
yet are remembered very clearly.

Settling of The Bride has much to say and learn,
has much to discover within the lifetimes of their relatives,
of how they were when in their youth,
when they were growing up,
when prior to the younger ones of the
next generations,
being present and accountable.

Settling of The Bride has aspects,
if of the farming genre,
varying with the sunrise and the sunset,
the daily life of farmers who must milk the cows or goats;
or be attentive to the crops of reliance and of nurture;
or to the herds of deer or beef,
or the flocks of mutton:
in the feeding of the grass and hay in season
with attention all year round.

Settling of The Bride varies with the age groups as evident within mortality,
as evident with the status of each purse,
or with the accrual of the eternal gold of God.

Settling of The Bride seeks experience in becoming accustomed:
to the means of transport,
to the feeding galleries,
to the non sequitur of sleep,
to the presence of the strangers and those within
what were the secret enclaves—
comprising those who gathered from the distant stars.

Settling of The Bride forestalls the arguments of nations,
the bickering of families,
the bartering of advantages,
the stepping out onto the fire-field of the battle with
the armouring of God.
Beware the sword of Vengeance as it is seized and swung.

Settling of The Bride approaches with restraint,
defers with orders to retreat.

Settling of The Bride measures and selects,
weighs and so defines,
dries and so compiles,
the internal aspects of the households of God,
the internal measurements of The Hosts of Heaven,
as summoned to play their part within the well-being of God.

Settling of The Bride is forever different from life within mortality,
is forever different from the means of existence within mortality,
is forever different from the mistakes of man within mortality,
is forever different from the justice meted out by man within mortality,
is forever different from the satanic castigations with the hangers-on as encountered within mortality.

Settling of The Bride has confidence in the sinecure of eternity,
has confidence in the security of the accountability of eternity,
has confidence in the semblances of The Holy Spirit:
to maintain the order and decorum—
essential to the workings of the throne rooms of God.

Settling of The Bride carries out and sustains,
upholds and mystifies,
marks and withdraws the task force of the majors and the minors;
modifies the mix of strength and weakness within the task forces of the vulnerable yet careless;
practices and alerts the volunteers,
yet experienced,
within the task forces of the warriors and the brave:
who go and do,
who do neither hesitate nor flinch,
who do neither re-examine nor appeal on what has gone before.

Settling of The Bride builds and strengthens The Edifice of God:
harmonizes and supports The Officers and The Administrators of God;
greets and welcomes The Princes and The Princesses of God;
rewards and honours The Kings and The Queens of God—
to all which has been promised stored or supplied or shared."

My Content Study Aid

Inheritance of The Bride

The End-time Testimonies of God

And I hear God The Father saying,
"Inheritance of The Bride does not consist of wishes,
is not satisfied by desires,
is hidden from the thieves and robbers of The Earth.

Inheritance of The Bride are the promises and the gifts of God,
where the result is intermingled on the gown of life,
where the jewels were saved and kept out of the reach of access from mortality.

Inheritance of The Bride is the rewards of God for taskings well completed,
for bearing all which was and is involved,
for overcoming the impediments to success,
for the achieving of the end result as decreed by God.

Inheritance of The Bride rests within the promised land—
for both The Jew and The Gentile,
where friction is non-existent,
where acceptance is the mode of governance.

Inheritance of The Bride builds in Faith,
recuperates in Grace;
is supported by The Spirit of My Son as He dwells within mortality,
in The Temples so assigned.

Inheritance of The Bride was born upon the cross of sacrifice,
upon the cross of redemption of the sin fields of man,
upon the cross of man where the man of man met with
the man of God,
where The Earth was marked by being enfolded by Heaven,
as reconciliation saw both the light of day and the darkness
of the void—
coming together to embrace with restoration:
the relationship of man and God prior to being
fractured within The Garden,
through the snake of Lucifer.

Inheritance of The Bride can grow and develop throughout mortality,
can grow and develop as maturity is attained,
can grow and develop as taskings are completed and lives
are changed under the influence of God.

Inheritance of The Bride is the memory of miracles as witnessed after prayer.

Inheritance of The Bride is in the presence of the miracles—
through the proxy ministry as authorised by God.

Inheritance of The Bride is the desires of the heart as granted by God.

Inheritance of The Bride is a close relationship with God,
is the receipt of The Gifts of The Spirit,
is the reality of The Gift of Tongues,
is the surrendering of Freewill in the procedures of binding
and of loosing,
where interruptions are invited as counselling is offered,
where wisdom is instated as The Tongues of Heaven become fluent,
on the tongue of man,
where the consideration of man is required to prepare The Way of
The Lord,
for it to apply to,
to be absorbed by,
each growing relationship with man and his Freewill.

Inheritance of The Bride is not the partial one where milk is forever served,
but rather the full and vibrant count of a meat dish:
served so understanding dawns and commitment is
deepened ever deeper,
as man matures in his thought life,
to adopt a life of Righteousness by the body,
and of Truth by the tongue.

Inheritance of The Bride is not shallow and trite,
which can be easily ignored,
where his shadow does not stop,
but just walks on by without any hesitation.

Inheritance of The Bride is deep and thought provoking,
is in earnest,
is worthwhile,
is rewarding,
is intriguing,
is interesting,
is a new beginning,
is a measuring of success within the mortal preparatory
walk with God.

Inheritance of The Bride,
when claimed in its fullness,
puts the seal upon eternity,
sets advancement into the university of God,
puts The Kings and Queens into the various fields of preparation,
for absorption of the details which puts royalty upon the thrones,
as perception increases,
as judgment is both sound and secure,

all as acquired from within the household of God—
as under the jurisdiction of The Living Loving God of man.

Inheritance of The Bride neither includes the idols nor the idolatry of man,
where belief is completely and utterly misplaced,
where eternity remains with the default,
where both Faith and Grace are not partnered for salvation,
as an end-time mystery remaining unattributed to God.

Inheritance of The Bride is knowledge which is teachable.

Inheritance of The Bride brings security of tenure,
brings Security of belief where Righteousness prevails,
brings Trust where Truth augments the conversations,
brings relief and thankfulness to the ending of each day.

Inheritance of The Bride does not fumble,
does not misapply,
does not bring forth that which is evil—
in either its nature or intent,
in either its presence or surroundings,
in either as a keepsake or as a souvenir from a visit in the past.

Inheritance of The Bride should be one of happiness and continual anticipation,
should be one of exploring with the relatives—
all the ins and outs with their cans and can'ts,
should be one of investigating where curiosity reigns and
the plumb lines are always true.

Inheritance of The Bride will always be remembered:
within the time frames and the seasons of the relatives,
so established now with footprints in eternity,
so established now with children lost too soon,
where children could not survive all that they encountered in the days of illness,
of hunger,
of cold,
with the continual worried looks of parents,
as they trudged to and from the church yard,
with its newly needed graves.

Inheritance of The Bride is being able to see the perfecting of the angels in attendance,
with the babes in arms who new very little in their time upon The Earth,
except that they were very close to God when gladness beamed,
for they wanted it to stay that way;
so all was well in the Heavenly Eternity as the angels were put in charge—
to keep it all just so."

Marshalling of The Bride

The End-time Testimonies of God

And I hear God The Father saying,
"Marshalling of The Bride takes organisational skills for the numbers as committed.

Marshalling of The Bride requires close attention being paid,
requires close attention with forbearance,
requires close attention to the need being defined.

Marshalling of The Bride requires needs to be realized,
needs to be summarised,
needs to become achievements,
needs for conversion to the approved and known,
needs to be set for the testified under servanthood,
needs of The Loving and The Kind,
needs of The Stationary with a history of observation,
needs of The Busy and Involved.

Marshalling of The Bride is not physical within mortality,
becomes apparent under the supernumeraries within the fields of choice,
where the onset of the gathering subsumes the space of ages.

Marshalling of The Bride is thorough and consistent,
is thoughtful and expeditious,
is enclosed and facilitated.

Marshalling of The Bride easily achieves the needs:
of matching up the allocations of accommodation—
as promised and prepared—
as announced by the intuitiveness of perception to the tongue experiences:
with the varying degrees of preparation towards the goal of fluency,
as spread among The Gathered.

Marshalling of The Bride,
where tongues were incomplete,
met with the loud speakers dependent on the ears,
to be moved as requested:
into the cycling apportionment of attribution,
with the guides and stewards of the streaming day,
who took their associates in hand to lead them,
to where they would be comfortable,
to settle in to the places as prepared.

Marshalling of The Bride attends to the group demonstrations of recharging,
as they are invited to partake of their meals.

Marshalling of The Bride checks to ensure all are fully satisfied,
in readiness to retire with assimilation to the fore.

Marshalling of The Bride has a time of composite investigation,
where each can wander on discovery,
where they can seek and find their ways,
where they have the new experiences previously unencountered,
where they can assess the new senses and effectiveness,
which they had not had before.

Marshalling of The Bride recognises that their eyes can see,
that their ears can hear,
that their brain can think—
to easily interact with others in the quietness of surroundings,
where the tongue no longer necessarily contributes to the power
of speech,
nor to the deliberate tasting of the food.

Marshalling of The Bride structures and installs,
motivates and encourages,
listens and responds.

Marshalling of The Bride is not on-going,
is not over-bearing,
is not over-reaching.

Marshalling of The Bride seeks the orderly and the forthright,
seeks familiarity with the blessings now at hand,
seeks companionship on all aspects of humanity,
now within God's Edifice of Eternity,
wherein The Saints of God do dwell.

Marshalling of The Bride inspects and checks for dissatisfaction,
in the early days of residence,
in the early days of observing with follow-ups on queries,
on the operating sequences of equipment,
designed to service the needs of the inhabitants.

Marshalling of The Bride ends just as quickly as it started,
removes the barriers from the difficult,
instructs and stays near-by for evidence of understanding,
with an enhanced capability to operate satisfactorily,
so no-one becomes stranded nor in need of rescuing.

Marshalling of The Bride meets the snowfields head-on,
enjoys great joy in the capturing of the slopes,
to travel them at speed.

Marshalling of The Bride spends time relaxing on the lakes of ice,
where speed and games are cautiously approached until experience is gained,
whereupon speed increases in leaps and bounds,
as spectators gather to watch the frolics:
with the surpassing speed achieved,
as races so require.

Marshalling of The Bride splits in divisions when visiting the seashores:
of the lapping waves,
of the taller waves which start to curl,
of the monster waves which enclose,
to capture out of sight,
to then shoot out with a whoosh,
with a thrill attached.

Marshalling of The Bride witnesses the camaraderie of souls,
the camaraderie of the related sibling sets,
the camaraderie of both discovery and bonding,
the camaraderie as the generational relationships
link hands to celebrate the onset of friendship,
as acquaintances quickly become the friends
of stature and significance.

Marshalling of The Bride opens a day of absence,
opens a day of dismissal,
opens a day where service and awareness are both attended
to and absorbed,
as the children play together in scenarios quite different and surprising,
as the marshalling of The Bride terminates in peace and tranquility,
before the throngs now moving:
within the backing of eternity,
within the presence of The Loving God."

My Content Study Aid

Reaching for The Bride

The End-time Testimonies of God

And I hear God The Father saying,
"Reaching for The Bride of My Son is a sign of acceptance and of approval of all My Son has said and done.

Reaching for The Bride is an attempt to come to know them better,
to come into their aura of existence,
to come into their reality while dwelling in Mortality.

Reaching for The Bride is an encouragement for preparation in its fullest,
for the knowledge base to be imparted,
for the wisdom to be granted to The Seekers
as consolidators of position.

Reaching for The Bride supports the integrity of The Trinity of God,
supports the interest taken in each constituent member,
for the achieving of success,
supports the approaching time frame:
by when preparation needs to be completed,
by when Fluency in Tongues is about to be put to use,
by when The Rhythm of The Saints will come into the
widening of significance,
both to send and to receive.

Reaching for The Bride completes the encircling of The Cross,
completes the gathering of The People as known by My Son,
completes their willingness and obedience in satisfying the
completeness of their preparation,
completes My purpose in submitting My Son as a sacrifice upon
The Cross,
as being the means of reconciliation of man with his God,
completes the end-time activities of God found as presented,
within the bounds of Faith with Grace.

Reaching for The Bride confirms their insight and perception,
into their progression beyond mortality.

Reaching for The Bride is an encouragement to one and all,
is an encouragement to enter through the gateway of acceptance,
is an encouragement to join in the future of The Family of God.

Reaching for The Bride speaks of The Father offering approval for commitment
built on Faith,
speaks of The Father satisfied with the outcome of The Cross,
speaks of The Father rejoicing at the out-turn of the days
of Pentecost:
among The New Believers as The Followers in Faith.

Reaching for The Bride explains to The Difficult and to The Insincere,
explains to The Volatile and The Fluctuating,
explains to The Anxious and The Compromised.

Reaching for The Bride searches and investigates,
acknowledges and welcomes,
invites and adopts into a family of renown.

Reaching for The Bride dispels the odours of iniquity,
dispels the scent of charlatans,
dispels the smells attached to the evil presences,
who would linger at a site subject to tuition.

Reaching for The Bride is an all-encompassing objective,
is an entirety complete,
is The Freewill attached and linked to an eternity,
where freedom reigns under the auspices of The Father.

Reaching for The Bride is the introductory part of establishing the welcome home,
of establishing the memory profiles of the distant past,
of establishing the history of life within Mortality,
of establishing the effectiveness of the preparation,
for a communicating sense to be dominant:
so it may fully serve new life within Eternity.

Reaching for The Bride sustains aspects of Mortality,
sustains knowledge and wisdom previously attained,
sustains confidence and acumen,
sustains perception with intelligent presumption,
sustains the combinational aspects of a character,
which recognizes all the joy and happiness achieved,
with their reasons for occurrence,
in the passing camelcade of life.

Reaching for The Bride encourages the climbers to reach up to the mountain peaks,
to overcome and to succeed,
to conquer and to cleanse:
the mountains from the lies and all means of deceit,
the mountains from their greed and all shades of
unwillingness to share,
the mountains with their routes to ease both their journeys

up and their journeys down:
with no sign of what is likely to be thrown or strewn
upon the mountain scape,
rather than to be carried home,
to not be left behind,
to not so taint the eyes,
with that which they would be
forced to see.

Reaching for The Bride negates the earthquakes of default,
the windstorms of disasters,
the wave forms of the turbulence which attacks
and overcomes.

Reaching for The Bride negates the intrusion of The Candles of The Lord,
negates the shrinkage of The Sun Fields,
negates the expansion of The Snow Fields,
negates the expansion of siphoned flow from within the rivers:
returning fish-dwelling water to the seas.

Reaching for The Bride seeks Love with Grace conquering lust,
seeks Love with Grace overcoming sin,
seeks Love with Grace welcoming 'Shalom'*:
throughout and at both ends of the length of day.

Reaching for The Bride extends the hand of God:
as it reaches into the affairs of man,
as it seeks to uphold The Love of The Father,
as it seeks to empower the onward move of man,
to where Eternity awaits within The Gardening of God."

Scribal Note: **Shalom – Peace, tranquility, wholeness, completeness, health, wealth, prosperity, favour. The ability to finish. To be safe. Nothing missing. Nothing broken. Nothing damaged.*

My Content Study Aid

____

____

____

____

____

____

____

Calling to The Bride to Come

The End-time Testimonies of God

And I hear God The Father saying,
Calling to The Bride to come should bring The Bride onto her knees,
should bring The Bride into her element,
should bring The Bride in readiness for adaption.

Calling to The Bride to come hears no clamour in response,
hears no rush of feet,
sees no peering crowd belonging to The Saints.

Calling to The Bride to come encounters no one listening for a trumpet call,
no one eagerly searching for the ways and means,
no one counting off the timing of a clock.

Calling to The Bride to come needs a better means of contact,
needs an affirmation of thought capability,
needs the installing of a new two way telephone exchange,
to liven up the circuitry to the instantaneous,
with security and non-interruptibility.

Calling to The Bride to come is not to instigate a rapture borne of deceit,
is not to bring a queue to the foreground,
is not to witness pushing and shoving as priority is claimed.

Calling to The Bride to come speaks of being ready to take the first step forward,
speaks of the time of preparation fast dwindling
into obscurity,
speaks of an unseemly panic by the majority in the fear of
being left behind.

Calling to The Bride to come initiates a rush dependent on a rumour,
initiates a crush against a fence with pushing from the back,
initiates and marks a showing of a lack of care and concern,
for those who appear to be the young,
the elderly—
those who are usually the most at risk when crowd
scenes move en masse,
as escape becomes impossible and breathing
very difficult.

Calling to The Bride to come leaves The Hearing with a stunned look of surprise,
marks The Ill-prepared with a face which speaks a
question mark,
as to where lies the way forward;
surprises some who did not know the voice of God,

yet assumed the stance with others of a watch and wait,
where expectations are almost non-existent.

Calling to The Bride to come is the faith call to The Multitudes,
is the reminder to The Procrastinators,
is the abjuring of the dilly-dallying so progress may proceed,
with righteous Faith to so be fulfilled.

Calling to The Bride to come is the truth call to join hands within eternity,
the answer awaited anxiously by the angels,
the decision of commitment which rewards the striving
of integrity,
within the morality of mortality.

Calling to The Bride to come is the call awaiting a response,
is the call of the utmost importance to every soul upon
The Earth,
is the call for which the spirit has been waiting,
for an acceptance as the basis of a relationship fulfilled.

Calling to The Bride to come should not be ignored,
should not be discarded because of a lack of understanding,
should not be the subject of denial,
when measured by all which lies in store in a future,
built upon the companionship of God.

Calling to The Bride to come upsets all demonic activity:
has them out in droves,
attempts to stop the invitations going out before it is too late.

Calling to The Bride to come has inundations from the lies of centuries,
has impressions from non-godly sources,
has nightmares to say such is not so—
as bound by the fields of horror and uncertainty.

Calling to The Bride to come attempts to bring a wave of confusion:
among the groups of the immoral,
among the gatherings of the God deniers,
among those involved with astrology—
together with the demonic interpretations
of the star fields in the sky,
among the fortune tellers with the cards concerned with destiny,
accompanied by words contributing to lies of evil intent—
all where easy money is the pitch from The Uncertain and The Curious,
from The Distraught in need of comforting,
from The Gullible and The Giggly where
every day brings forth a party,
or a tattoo encroaching on the very likeness of God.

Calling to The Bride to come should be answered without undue delay,
should be either confirmed or affirmed,
as the case may be,
with an intent arising from integrity:
where the future destiny,
as described and brought to attention,
has real meaning filled with joy and relaxation,
has a future within the very environs of God,
with all He has prepared for the jubilant and
the accepting,
within the time frame of preparation—
as evidenced within the bounds of mortality.

Calling to The Bride to come will not surprise the sheep with their lambs,
will cause heads to be uplifted,
will cause frolicking at large,
will bring certainty to a destiny of choice,
will bring meaning with understanding of The Pentecostal
Gifts of God.

Calling to The Bride to come surpasses,
in importance,
all other calls to man,
all other components of The New Covenant on offer,
all that was instated at The Cross
for the sacrificial reconciliation,
for an ongoing life with The Trinity of God:
The Living Loving Three-in-one as The Entity of Godly Presence—
within The Temples of The Life of Man."

My Content Study Aid

Encouraging The Bride-to-be

The End-time Testimonies of God

And I hear God The Father saying,
"Encouraging The Bride-to-be leaves open the door for invitations,
leaves the door ajar for others to follow in the stead,
leaves each soul following the leading of the spirit,
with the approval of a guiding authority now accepted,
as the way to go forward as the spirit counsels.

Encouraging The Bride-to-be offers a flow chart for success,
offers the matured wisdom of the ages,
offers the gifts of The Spirit of God as bequeathed
at Pentecost.

Encouraging The Bride-to-be has many different starting points,
has many misconceptions in need of correction or rejection,
has many different sources from which to draw a concept
of a god,
which is almost certainly in error.

Encouraging The Bride-to-be requires an open mind which is The Seeker of The Truth,
which has a capacity for Faith well placed,
so to be watered as it grows,
to have an initial mentor who can answer the questions which arise,
from within the thought processes of The New Born Lambs of God.

Encouraging The Bride-to-be is to concentrate on the followers rather than the scouts,
is to settle on the leadership without the quitters and
the questioners,
who cannot accept instructions,
is to be forthright and non-excusable where responsibility
is seen to rest on shoulders.

Encouraging The Bride-to-be is the targeting of objectives,
is the not looking at the past,
is the settling for the best and all that that implies.

Encouraging The Bride-to-be is presence at the gatherings,
is participation is assembling,
is the communicating of desires and dreams and visions,
as encountered by the day and by the night.

Encouraging The Bride-to-be expands and multiplies,
informs and transmits,
understands and practices,
The Proxy Healing Ministries of God.

Encouraging The Bride-to-be sees the joining of the threads,
sees the effort evidenced in acquisition of the truth,
sees the knowledge base expanding as the teachers teach,
to follow up on any puzzled faces,
sees the smiles of satisfaction
as the penny drops on understanding,
as memory is reinforced with The Worthwhile
and The Valued.

Encouraging The Bride-to-be has summations of achievement,
has progress reflected in the growth,
has testimonies born as certainty confirms the concepts:
as they arise to be tested for either acceptance or rejection,
within the fields of Grace,
of Truth,
of Righteousness,
as The Temples of The Spirit select and address
The Incumbent and The Spread-eagled,
in the seeking of a relationship with their new-found God.

Encouraging The Bride-to-be is serving meat up to accompany the milk,
to ensure both are measured meaningfully,
as well as carefully,
so neither goes to waste.

Encouraging The Bride-to-be witnesses enthusiasm repaying involvement,
witnesses Truth replacing hesitations,
witnesses confidence expressing certainty with
Righteousness displayed.

Encouraging The Bride-to-be does not muddy the clean water,
does not contaminate purity with the unclean,
does not get lost in fog when the eyes lose their glow
of concentration,
as the soul is seen to wander.

Encouraging The Bride-to-be functions best when there the heart enjoys
a filling of commitment,
a filling of an imparted viewing of the future built with God,
a filling of The Spirit bringing relay station transfers of
thoughts and possibilities,
as fluency of the tongue masters all that is expected,
so advancement is assured,
as interpretation follows.

Encouraging The Bride-to-be is a dipping into the self-help basket,
of sharing and of discussion,
of inspection and of evaluation,

of memory and decisiveness,
as families are seen to benefit from the positive and the rewarding,
as simplicity fails to argue with the complex and uncertain.

Encouraging The Bride-to-be knows:
of confidence expressed,
of smiles seen lighting up the faces,
of the children filled with happiness as the environment
is changed.

Encouraging The Bride-to-be sees eagerness in action,
sees thoughts expressed with maturity,
sees the scriptures applied and bringing change.

Encouraging The Bride-to-be lifts and circulates,
harnesses and sets free,
modifies and improves the lifestyles of The Found,
the habitations of The Blessed,
the purses filled with wisdom,
and with plenty that goes much further than before.

Encouraging The Bride-to-be has a payday with The Bride,
has a merging of the two,
has The Charitable and The Fulfilled leaving
the unkept and the selfish far behind in their wake.

Encouraging The Bride-to-be has birthdays based on Christmas,
has gifts based on Pentecost,
has Love and Truth and Righteousness as The Harbinger
of Peace.

Encouraging The Bride-to-be sees the angels rejoicing in their messaging,
sees the butterflies of heaven in all their beauty as they come to Earth,
sees the footsteps of The Committed following others on the sands of time:
which lead into Eternity within The Adopted Family of God."

My Content Study Aid

Separating of The Bride

The End-time Testimonies of God

And I hear God The Father saying,
"Separating of The Bride is the goal for purity of lifestyle,
is the goal for unity of purpose,
is the goal of the quest for eternal life well served,
as accompanied by the integrity of the body soul and spirit.

Separating of The Bride sees the insincere departing,
sees the tares weeded from the grains,
sees the liars unaccepted because of their Freewill misapplied,
sees the failures to comply with the preparation as required,
settled into the physicality of the immoral mortal world at large.

Separating of The Bride sees The Undefiled through Grace
chosen for their new found freedom,
sees The Understanding and The Committed
following on the pathway of discipleship,
sees The Families,
The Lonely,
The Cognizant of The Church of God,
all prepared for seeking shelter under the wings of God,
under the adoptive care of God,
under the ongoing faith in,
fealty to,
fear of,
The Living Loving God of all creation
as visible on and from The Earth,
while travelling both through time and space.

Separating of The Bride does not come without due warning of the consequences,
of the change in destination when standards are not met,
of the loss of freedom as accountability is incurred,
so to be upheld as justice is applied.

Separating of The Bride gives ample time for preparation when eagerness is shown,
when application is evident,
when the prayer field is besieged
with requests and queries:
by a new found lamb.

Separating of The Bride will progress under the timed schedule of God
in the time driven world of man.

Separating of The Bride is neither a time of hustle nor of fluster,

of showcasing nor of flouncing,
of comparison nor of comment.

Separating of The Bride achieves The Will of God,
ensures sin is left where it belongs,
farewells the hangers-on with those attempting to curry favour,
welcomes such in surroundings as equipped
for and with The Love of God.

Separating of The Bride sees the gathering of The Temples of The Spirit,
as the clusters grow and meld,
as The Committed and The Enthusiastic all combine together,
as the voices of thousands are heard to rise in adoration of The Semblance,
in affirmation of situation,
in worship of their King.

Separating of The Bride locates the independent from The Dependant,
locates the ill-prepared from The Fluent and The Ready,
locates the time free in their procrastination,
from The Time Aware meeting in decisiveness.

Separating of The Bride sees expectations rise,
sees adjustments made to clothing,
sees faces in the mirrors.

Separating of The Bride has to-do lists seen to be unfolding,
has note taking seen to be multiplying,
has grooming coming to the centre stage as presentation rises
in importance.

Separating of The Bride sees The Hobblers and The Limping using their favourite means
of support,
sees The Wheel Chairs out in front,
in preferring the smooth from the rugged,
with the setting of positions.

Separating of The Bride witnesses the crowds diminishing,
as selections continue at the interface of man with God,
where wishing in hope has comparison,
as it encounters Faith in action.

Separating of The Bride sees families bond together,
sees families gathered in prayer,
sees families familiar with one another in their quests:
for reaching out to Eternity within The Presence of God.

Separating of The Bride leaves many questions on the lips,
leaves many thoughts unspoken,
leaves many relationships in tatters as all hope is lost,
as morality is questioned far too late—
to have any worthwhile effect upon Freewill.

Separating of The Bride indicates those who have The Trust of God,
those who know their God,
those who converse with their God,
those who honoured The Pentecostal Gifts,
those who qualified through Grace.

Separating of The Bride removes the causes of uncertainty,
the causes of the gossip,
the causes of the lies,
the causes of carried sin,
the causes of immorality,
the causes of wayward behaviour without the fear of God.

Separating of The Bride highlights the best in man,
highlights the slothfulness of man,
highlights the unjustified expectations of man,
highlights the proxy ministries and taskings from The Lord Jesus,
in His Wisdom and His Agapé.

Separating of The Bride puts enlightened ministry into the future walk with God,
puts fresh energy into preparatory exposure to The Gift of Tongues,
with the quest for fluency in The Temples of The Spirit.

Separating of The Bride forever changes circumstances of The Beloved of God,
forever changes access to The Gates of Eternity,
forever changes life episodes within the grandest of grand settings,
forever honours all that God has prepared,
forever brings Eternity into the reality of man."

My Content Study Aid

Multitudes within The Bride

The End-time Testimonies of God

And I hear God The Father saying,
"Multitudes within The Bride are welcomed to advance,
are welcomed to contribute,
are welcomed to so merge
into the mosaic of The Bride of My Son.

Multitudes within The Bride are a positive release within the gathering of The Bride,
stretch the prospects wide and clear for assimilation within Eternity,
concentrate the traits and the values opened for sharing and exploration.

Multitudes within The Bride bring their national customs of where they were bound,
prior to release into the freedom of the skies.

Multitudes within The Bride enjoy a new found Freedom based on truth and realization,
based on confidence and certainty of commitment,
have homes where discernment is assured,
where the young at heart have a new direction,
in their approach and attitude to life.

Multitudes within The Bride share the colours and the cuts of their clothing;
their ways of dressing and of celebrating the worthwhile and the loved;
the acquisitions of the gifts of God waiting patiently
for fluency to be attained;
as fresh relay stations become active and sustained,
as The Temples of God graduate into maturity,
with The Guest who comes to stay.

Multitudes within The Bride approach and introduce;
exchange questions and answers as understanding dawns—
upon the positioning of privacy revealed;
appreciate and remember the new standards of growth
and friendship,
within the camaraderie of companionship acquired.

Multitudes within The Bride bump into those behind,
offer apologies of profuseness,
attempt to make amends with the new conversationalists
however they are introduced.

Multitudes within The Bride attempt to reach out to the standards of The Bride,
to assimilate and adopt with appreciation those made
known to be declared,
in the living testimonies of what has surely come to be.

Multitudes within The Bride are seen to merge and feel at home,
are seen to discuss and to adopt,
are seen to polish and admire the tongue within the mouth.

Multitudes within The Bride learn the songs of praise,
of redemption,
of salvation,
of worship,
of The Kingdom,
of The King,
of Eternity at large.

Multitudes within The Bride hurry to be included,
hurry to be worthy,
hurry to be fluent,
hurry to be taught the wonders and the signs,
the miracles and proxy ministries—
of all that God would have them do.

Multitudes within The Bride do not waste the moments of personal relationship,
do not waste the moments of personal counselling,
do not waste the timed frames where the heavens do declare:
to the spirit and the soul in their walks of life
within mortality.

Multitudes within The Bride develop an appreciation for The Groom of valour,
for The Groom of Kingship,
for The Groom as destined to reign
within His Kingdom in partnership with The Elect of God—
those who followed in His footsteps,
as well as by His example,
in following through the waters of the second birth.

Multitudes within The Bride realize the significance of the third birth through the grave.

Multitudes within The Bride do not vacate and turn away,
do not surrender to the difficulties and hardships as
encountered in the troughs,
do not get carried away by the high points of achievement,
where the power and the authority of God is everywhere displayed,
to all with a personal relationship with God,
with Faith in Healing as resulting from the welcomed prayer of Faith,
where healings and gifts do confirm The Reality of God:
in the lives of those who would so testify of such,
to await in confidence for the end results.

Multitudes within The Bride watch over carefully their Freewill agency:
as to how it is applied,
with the results therefrom.

Multitudes within The Bride should fully understand and comprehend,
the importance of The Application of Freewill,
of how it is evaluated,
of how the scales of justice are weighted,
of how the destiny of default
or the destiny of choice are the ones to be determined:
as the end result of a life just lived in immorality yet respected,
or a life well spent within the sight of God,
to be so honoured,
with its days within The Adopted Family of God.

Multitudes within The Bride are led to the stairways of the stars,
the stairways controlling the jump-off points,
on journeys of exploration and discovery,
within the systems awaiting visits opening
eyes and ears—
to the cascades of delivery,
to the thunder and the lightning as never seen before,
to the water falls and turbulence as shared
in locations,
from where The Son light holds full sway,
from where the vistas with their scents and music
speak of places never seen before,
in any place upon The Earth.

Multitudes within The Bride attend the schools of learning,
attend the universities of God,
attend the level playing fields where all are treated equally;
as they share in all the opportunities as seen to be available,
with neither fear nor favour,
nor jealousy nor pride,
will surface to decry the effort as applied,
together with the garland as awarded.

Multitudes within The Bride swell and develop as knowledge gains a foothold,
as wisdom gains the ascendancy,
as the goals contribute to all which is to be sought,
to be carried by the spirits and the souls,
as Truth and Integrity are seen to flourish with Righteousness:
within the fields of Peace and Harmony;
where Justice rules with Honesty and Mercy,
as rendered by their Living Loving God of all Eternity and Space."

Testifying of The Would-be-Bride

The End-time Testimonies of God

And I hear God The Father saying,
"Testifying of the would-be Bride brings attention to The Novice,
brings acceptance to The Initiate,
brings immersion baptism to The Committed and Sincere.

Testifying of the would-be Bride garners and replenishes,
fills and overflows,
welcomes the gifts of Pentecost,
ascribes to the empowering of Freewill,
where accountability borders all horizons,
where accountability amends all broken promises,
where accountability calls up the encountered forces designed to search,
to strip,
to take—
for which reparation is to be required.

Testifying of the would-be Bride sees attitudes in a state of flux,
sees attitudes changing with due emphasis,
sees lifestyles willing to accept,
to uphold the parameters as set by God.

Testifying of the would-be Bride brings thinking to the fore,
brings feelings as exposed,
brings consideration of all which is involved,
in accepting Righteousness and Truth,
as the two twins intertwined within The Love of God:
as they bring Peace and Happiness to the landscape,
holding the sanctuaries of My People,
as tranquility is seeded to take root,
as its time of flowering develops,
within the springtime of hope and change.

Testifying of the would-be Bride declares the inner heart afresh,
overwrites through Grace the demeanours of the past:
where apologies were mislaid—
to never see the light of day.

Testifying of the would-be Bride has no need to be a recounting of the past,
has no need to splash the mire onto a mirror,
has no need to become a recitation of past deeds
now regretted—
as all are already known to God,
as left upon The Cross with its New Covenant in place.

Testifying of the would-be Bride does not have as an objective:
the scratching of the itches,
the raising of a rash,
the opening of a wound of shame—
of that which has been treated,
to now be sealed upon the lips of forgiveness,
of healing,
to now be waylaid for permanent discarding under The Grace of God.

Testifying of the would-be Bride does neither recall nor revisit the vomit of the past.

Testifying of the would-be Bride is in the here and now,
is in the new concepts being learnt,
the new concepts being applied,
the new concepts introducing first hand experience:
of The Agapé and The Security of God;
for a fresh starting point for all awaiting in Eternity with The God of Love,
as detailed for the management and guidance counselling,
of each life seen to be sheltering under His all encompassing umbrella,
as held erect within the far-reaching mantle of The Living God.

Testifying of the would-be Bride rubs no salt into a wound,
uses no pumice stone upon the healed,
does not attack a scab so the underside reveals all,
which has so far been retained,
which has so far failed to heal,
which has so far not seen the light of forgiveness,
nor has the puss been overcome.

Testifying of the would-be Bride should place all the troubles into a placid sea,
where the waves have only cause to lap gently on the shore line,
where the summer sun makes all warm and welcome:
to bathe within The ongoing Love of God.

Testifying of the would-be Bride is the golden opportunity to bring glory to The Son,
that He in His wisdom may bring Glory to The Father.

Testifying of the would-be Bride creates a testimony bubbling in the soul,
to be recounted by the spirit,
in the harmony of The Temple:
where The Guest has been invited,
to be well bedded in,
to check and to know the degree of purity attained,
in the time of preparation;
with the degree of fluency of The Tongues of Heaven,
as they fall upon,
in utterance,
on the tongue of man.

Testifying of the would-be Bride is a requirement of The Lord Jesus—
to testify of Him:
so He may testify before The Father,
of all The Son's would-be sheep within His fold.

Testifying of the would-be Bride has no reward for silence,
receives silence from The Son as He stands before The Father;
without a testimony of all that Faith and Trust has achieved,
through His sacrifice upon The Cross.

Not testifying by the would-be Bride leaves the tongue silent,
in the silence of the destiny of default,
through non-qualification,
as the goat is unmasked from behind an intrusion,
where faith and knowledge are both unknown,
in lives which lead to the second death.

Testifying of the would-be Bride is an honour reserved:
for The Committed and The Worthy,
for The Lively and The Justified,
for The Valued and The Crowned of God:
as they live their lives in mortality,
with their Freewill marshalled and related,
to the ongoing of an eternal life
with the promises intact—
to so bear their fruit in due season,
within The Oversight and Agapé of God.

The end-time testimonies of God are prerequisites,
both ways,
for entry into His Kingdom,
under His eternal reign."

My Content Study Aid

Counting of The Sands of Time

The End-time Testimonies of God

And I hear God The Father saying,
"Counting of the sands of time have no meaningful descriptors when related to eternity,
do have meaningful descriptors when stationed temporarily,
within the passage of mortality.

Counting of the sands of time has no objective unless the clock of man is running,
has no results unless the time scale can be read,
has no real intrinsic value unless comparisons are valid.

Counting of the sands of time is a figurative analogy,
is not due for a literal interpretation,
yields no real understanding:
even when the numbers may be quoted,
even when seen to be so large that meaning is destroyed,
even when wisdom is under test,
as truth searches for an escape route,
which does not generate the onset of a lie.

Counting of the sands of time is a result of the milling of the waves,
of the grinding of the foreshore,
of the rolling of the stones still at large
with variability of weight,
as the tide approaches to so attempt to move all of the obstructions,
as collisions are created,
as splinters are broken off,
as the jagged and the sharp use momentum as a friendly patient force,
in disintegration of the shore—
seen acting as a back stop,
yet often overcome by the greediness
of the tide,
as it envelops to eventually lug away.

Counting of the sands of time is not a rewarding pastime for a beach without the input,
is not a pastime often seen in duplication,
is not a pastime often yielding stones of value,
with a sparkle hidden inside,
as each suspect is loathe to yield,
unless attention can be paid,
to the polishing,
the cut,
or the gluing to support.

Counting of the sands of time can build a table of the specimens,
a dish of the assorted,
a necklace of the provisioning of nature,
which has the credibility from the catching of the eye,
where tumble rumbling with carborundum,
then polishing with tin oxide on an old model ringer,
as sits above a washing machine,
with a tyre hung upon the ringer to revolve,
so a slurry,
over several days,
can put a glow into an approving eye:
for discoveries deemed worthwhile,
to be treated of some value,
for a gem stone as brought to life,
as examined both with amazement,
and with pride in satisfaction,
to so stand the test of time and solitude.

Counting of the sands of time do not vest in satisfaction,
rather speak of a wasting of potential,
of matters unsecured,
of items beyond control,
of the stake of interest not yielding
a worthwhile return.

Counting of the sands of time are best vanquished from the mind-set,
are best committed to another place and time,
are best held and kept beyond the windows of achievement,
for a bestowal of just a casual glance.

Counting of the sands of time has no end in sight,
has no verification of the total,
does not assert correctness as ever being achieved:
the error in encoding can stretch across divides,
can linger in a proximity,
can be disappointing in extremes.

Counting of the sands of time is best transferred to a more worthwhile activity,
of dealing with like for like,
of an analysis of wealth,
of progression within the field of knowledge,
of the assessment of the parameters which
are known to increase,
not absorb,
the cakewalk of man amongst the outpouring of success.

Counting of the sands of time lives in a glum face,
lives in the loneliness of possession,
lives in the trials and defeats,
so common among the inexperienced,
who are saddled with a load,
which is never lightened nor transformed,
into what others can admire.

Counting of the sands of time brings dejection to the fore,
records an extended time where the books no longer balance,
where the downhill slope is becoming steeper,
as a slither becomes a land slide out of all proportions,
ending in an uncouth lump at the bottom of what was once a garden,
free from weeds and rejected life.

Counting of the sands of time should be changed to a counting:
of the nodules of success,
of the bankable and accumulative,
of the worthwhile encouraging
of an attack upon fulfilment,
where the results are shouted in enjoyment,
as rewards bedeck the chest.

Counting of the sands of time never has,
nor had,
an endtime leading into a group of satisfied servants,
who wield the smoking guns,
where errors and assumptions affect the out-turn of success.

Counting of the sands of time does not yield any time,
as counted of significance,
as having value added,
of thereafter being sought and shared.

Counting of the sands of time is not the way as thought to be desirable,
is a mishmash of the plausible intertwined,
within that found to be just out of reach,
where sniggering is heard as corrections take their toll,
with uncertain outcomes as evidenced by the squandering:
of both the timing of the day and of the night."

My Content Study Aid

Meeting at The Banquet

The End-time Testimonies of God

And I hear God The Father saying,
"Meeting at the banquet can be a mass of introductions,
can be a searching for relationships,
can be a generator of hesitation built on insecurity.

Meeting at the banquet can require assimilation,
can require competence in languages,
can require fluency in The Tongues of God.

Meeting at the banquet is a test of preparation when in mortality,
is a test of the level of development of the sixth sense,
is a test put upon the memory as fully restored and operational.

Meeting at the banquet indicates a willingness to mingle,
a willingness to seek and find,
a willingness to accept,
to identify,
the positioning when seen to be at rest.

Meeting at the banquet has no functioning of cost,
has no launching of an appeal,
has no forming of a queue.

Meeting at the banquet is a fresh air experience,
is a combining of the interests,
is a gathering of intent,
is the circumstances being brought into effect from promises
instated many years ago.

Meeting at the banquet raises eyebrows in surprise,
raises voices in excitement when chosen to be used,
raises arms raised in gesticulation from a distance,
in the seeking of acknowledgement.

Meeting at the banquet is a joy unto The Gathered,
when fully prepared for all as expected,
with introductions to the fore,
as conversations impale upon the levels
of understanding.

Meeting at the banquet signifies acceptance on the grandest of grand scales,
signifies the proliferation of regeneration of all which
were requiring healing:
with replacement of the critical but lost,
signifies the welcome as widely spread and appreciated,

as widely prepared and put in place,
as widely encircling in reaching both the unknown,
and the puzzled faces where familiarity does not open
many possibilities,
as to the 'who' and 'when'.

Meeting at the banquet can change or add to the groupings of relationships,
can modify or qualify the approaches to strangers,
who may look familiar;
can edit or delete the pages built on memory,
where familiarity awaits a confirmation of identity.

Meeting at the banquet sees discussion points of centuries,
sees queries based on supposition,
where doubt and mystery still surround the history:
awaiting the fulfilment of revelatory enquiries,
sees the welcome flash of recognition as the penny drops into the
slot within a family tree.

Meeting at the banquet celebrates the works of God:
celebrates His preparations,
celebrates His planning and His foresight,
celebrates all the places as prepared and ready for the reception
of His temples.

Meeting at the banquet upholds and fulfills the promises of God,
lauds and holds dear the valued or the worshipful,
the jewels as assigned when in mortality for release on such a day,
when the angels are filled with delight and wearing smiles of ecstasy,
on seeing their people who were long ago committed to their care.

Meeting at the banquet is the highlight of reunion,
is the future of the promises arriving in the present,
is The Mortal Concept as held in Faith and Grace,
as now has come to pass,
as originating from The Cross of Sacrifice,
as now attained in maturity in holding the keys:
to immortality and life within Eternity,
as The Destiny of Choice now overshadows to fulfil,
all which has gone before in the gifting of Freewill.

For as the ages lapse,
so they are so named.
For as the ages carry to redeem,
so they survey their losses as incurred.
For as the ages promote man in his achievements,
so opportunity arises:
to survey the inlaid security of the field of Grace.

Meeting at the banquet creates stories in themselves,
creates sessions worth retelling,
creates memories no longer seen in conflict:
as Righteousness is seen to introduce Peace with Tranquility,
throughout The Kingdom of The Son.

Meeting at the banquet hears the singing of the angels,
in octaves thought to be completely out of reach,
witnesses the purity of fellowship available to all,
highlights the customs and endeavours of the heavens,
about to be instated at the transitioning of The Earth.

Meeting at the banquet establishes an interest in the history,
which mostly went unrecorded.

Meeting at the banquet left recharging fully sated,
left new languages being tested,
left familiarity with the new homes being acquired in the process
of settling in—
as both strange and joyful,
as comfort and needs are both found easy to assimilate,
with the presence as created by The Loving God.

Meeting at the banquet has no one missing out,
has no late arrivals,
has no misunderstandings—
arising from any concepts misconstrued.

Meeting at the banquet extends until sufficiency brings wisdom to the fore,
brings a willingness to attend as scheduled and expected,
brings the opportunity of choice with images,
inherent in the decision making process:
as to 'what' and 'when' and 'why' and 'how'.

Meeting at the banquet informs as to the protocols,
informs as to the culture formed afresh in replenishment,
informs in certainty of being of the morality of God,
where the ethics of man have neither use nor application."

My Content Study Aid

Love for Our People

The End-time Testimonies of God

And I hear God The Father saying,
"Love for our people includes all aspects of their lives,
includes all categories of pain and of misuse,
includes all concepts inherent in perceptions and assumptions,
includes all trials and errors as spent on the fields of Righteousness
and Truth.

Love for our people brings all to a central place,
brings all under The Mantel of Grace,
brings all into The Flock of God,
brings all into The Temples of The Spirit,
brings all to know The Ark of the New Covenant
and wherein it is found.

Love for our people has no time frame for expiry,
has no time frame for dissipation,
has no time frame for dismemberment.

Love for our people extends into mortality,
extends throughout eternity,
extends to every soul and spirit and body resulting from creation.

Love for our people is not embedded in idolatry,
is not empowered by the strands of evil,
is not affected by the climate of the day or night.

Love for our people is an ongoing systemic attribute of The God of Love,
reaches out in friendship in tolerance in Agapé,
in all aspects of life upon The Earth,
in all coverage of circumstances as found within the harnessing
of prayer,
in all the compilations where Grace resolves the difficulties,
as encountered from the drainpipes of iniquity,
as sin within mortality—
from the viewpoint,
with the moral proclamations,
of The Everlasting God of Love.

Love for our people includes the offering of reconciliation,
as borne by The Cross of Christ,
The Messiah as awaited and rejected through the
embitterment of our people,
where the temple of the period did not bring sanctification,
to the livelihood of man.

Love for our people surmounted the evil entities,
as presented in the hate fields of the satanic hordes,
who swayed and motivated the crowds beyond
any semblance of righteousness or of truth.

Love for our people was affirmed by the prayer of forgiveness:
as issuing on The Cross,
from the nailed body of My Son.

Love for our people is reciprocated by understanding and commitment,
by Wisdom and by Faith,
in gratitude and thanksgiving across the spread of worship and of acceptance:
within the heart-shielding of The Ark of The New Covenant,
within the dwelling places of The Temples of The Spirit,
within the knowledge base extending to The Grace Fields of Mortality—
next to those of Righteousness and Truth,
where Wisdom reigns within The Will of God.

Love for our people draws a circle with its circumference,
surrounding and sustaining each entity of being:
within the guiding light of angels,
within the confirming care of The Spirit,
within the vigour and reality of The Promises of God.

Love for our people is everywhere uplifting,
is everywhere displayed,
is everywhere in evidence by all which is supplied.

Love for our people covers as if a network of assimilation into The Family of God,
enhances their walk with God in discipleship,
accommodates the recalcitrants who,
in ignorance,
struggle to be free from the shelter of the empirical and the steadfast,
from the beauty for the eyes,
from the sounding for the ears,
from the touching for the feeling,
for the words of sensitivity of description,
of all that is encountered as available for expression,
by the tongue of man.

Love for our people guides and directs The Guardians of God:
the angelic bands,
the hosts of heaven,
the resurrected entities,
together with the cherubim,
the elders,
the winged—
all who dwell within the throne rooms of God,

as well as those in service of their God within The Edifice of God—
both in Heaven and upon The Earth.

Love for our people results in raised hopes and expectations,
results in increased enthusiasm and commitment,
results in increased purity within The Bride of My Son.

Love for our people holds tightly to the bounds of safety,
guards responsibly the outskirts of existence,
guards knowledgeably the travellers to and fro,
the renewers of the trails,
the investigators of the wellness,
of the presentability where joy and happiness are
the precursors and supporters of The Newly Entered,
into the eternal way of life.

Love for our people motivates the healing power and the proxy authority of God.

Love for our people motivates the availability and the wisdom sharing of our God.

Love for our people motivates the growth capabilities for the onward explorations,
of The Saints of God,
of The Martyrs of The Cross,
of the reaching out to The Multitudes
for their gathering,
in caring for the survivors of the
cleansing of The Earth—
where its shorelines are most vulnerable,
where its contamination is most common,
where the habitational capacity is most concentrated,
where the loss of life will be at its greatest,
where the white horse and its bowman will be releasing arrows,
with their messages to impact directly with their meaning,
on the selected hearts of man."

My Content Study Aid

Hesitancy of Our People

The End-time Testimonies of God

And I hear God The Father saying,
"Hesitancy of our people leaves procrastination wide open and ready to be used,
leaves delays as possible interruptions to the schedule
as installed,
leaves confusion in place as control is lost,
as it so waits for another day not booked elsewhere.

Hesitancy of our people leads into a daytime of uncertainty,
leads into a change as called in urgency,
leads into a shortage which needs to be replaced.

Hesitancy of our people vies with Time in short supply,
vies with Time not planned but wasted,
vies with Time in a welcomed change of priorities
as it leaves the past undone,
with an addition to the queue.

Hesitancy of our people should not become a way of life,
should not be practicing 'catch up' to the relevant and waiting,
should not be a juggler with the facts there for attention.

Hesitancy of our people must not breed diversions,
must not breed distractions,
must not breed infiltrators to contaminate objectives.

Hesitancy of our people should not dwell upon the timetable of others,
should not sleep when the cricket pitch is ready for attack,
should not seek the spirit in the bottle which is sealed,
yet still issues an invitation to take part.

Hesitancy of our people should not be drawn into a quorum of the failed,
should not try to find enlightenment among the blind and deaf,
should not seek wisdom in the darkness,
should not seek help from the impaired of intellect,
should not encroach with queries which are without significance,
should not reject the covering of Grace.

Hesitancy of our people should not arise from mixing right with wrong,
from suffering from a selective memory
with neither rhyme nor reason as a backstop,
from a muddying of the creek in which all
must eventually bathe their thoughts,
from relaxation in a spa where all thoughts touch
on the trivial while awaiting interference.

Hesitancy of our people should be supplanted by decision making,
should be overcome by decisiveness,
should be the target for despatch,
should be removed from consideration:
in leaving room for activities among the taskings
as offered by The God of Nations.

Hesitancy of our people is an adoption of the functioning of doubt,
is in the temporary absence of the grasp of Faith.

Hesitancy of our people should know what they should be doing,
should know the tasks worthy of achieving in a timely manner,
should know the confidence of achievement,
as progress marks off the approaching of maturity,
of completion,
of reporting all is well and understood.

Hesitancy of our people puts chaperones among the mingling crowd,
puts appraisers of intent among the planners
and resource managers,
puts the nosy where they should not be,
as they generate the gossip with exaggeration,
as they contribute very little which can be taken as reliable,
as they travel on their way mixing up and casting promises,
later failing for a lack of activity,
as such become the lies of retrospect and trial.

Hesitancy of our people is often as a result arising from a lacking of verification,
is often information later seen to be throwing doubt upon
that offered,
from the ignorant or the lazy who have listened to the gossip.

Hesitancy of our people should not settle to contaminate
the harmless beauty of the butterflies,
should not ignore the invasions of the wasps,
seen bringing stings unto the tables:
of constructive criticism;
of informed debate;
of qualified instruction;
of learned experience;
of training of relevance;
of an education borne of relevant study,
under teachers fully qualified,
in their areas of learning.

Hesitancy of our people need to know when to listen and acquire,
when to sit back and affirm,
when to lean forward and offer an informed opinion.

Hesitancy of our people must knock hesitancy upon its head,
must vanquish lack of detail,
must seek a greater knowledge base for acquisition with
reference points of reliability.

Hesitancy of our people are not there to wonder,
are not there to guess,
are not there to suppose,
are not there to imagine the unproven,
are not there to relate stories with no bearing
on the subject awaiting a solution,
from the informed and the experienced;
where the apprentice of deed and thought
should wait an invitation to contribute.

Hesitancy of our people should not prolong the drought,
where hesitation holds the floor,
in reciting irrelevancies from the past with no bearing
on the present.

Hesitancy of our people is not a good ending to a day,
is of serious concern at the closure of a week,
is a disaster at a month-end as progress grinds to a halt,
as silence reigns,
as a strike comes into effect
to frustrate matters even further.

Hesitancy of our people does not offer the certainty of a way forward,
is as a man groping in the darkness on a control panel of unfamiliarity,
where trial and error reigns and common sense is long forsaken."

My Content Study Aid

Future of Our People

The End-time Testimonies of God

And I hear God The Father saying,
"Future of our people have revelation to the fore,
have revelation flowing from My Prophets,
have revelation worthy of recording.

Future of our people can see to pick up pieces,
can see to gather what is considered valuable,
can see to accept the wisdom with the knowledge.

Future of our people is one of development with progress,
is one of sophistication with discovery,
is one of interpretation with understanding.

Future of our people rests upon initiative,
rests upon perception,
rests upon the learning from the past.

Future of our people will uplift the ability to progress,
the ability to explore,
the ability to remember and foresee,
the ability to dwell both within and beyond the catchment
sphere of time,
the ability to bring justice to the fore,
the ability to reinstate the falsely judged and mistreated.

Future of our people lies within The Fields of God,
lies within The Keys of The Kingdom,
lies within The Counselling of God,
lies with graduating from the university of Godly inspiration,
with abilities complete and active,
within their fields of study.

Future of our people does not encroach on neighbours,
does not inspect the private,
does not peer with a search light into darkness when under restraint.

Future of our people rejoice and celebrate at all they have achieved,
at all within the surroundings of the present,
at all as laid upon an altar:
for inviting access as it come to be.

Future of our people do neither hesitate nor vacillate,
do neither tend to the immoral nor to aspects of false doctrine,
do neither tend to immature truth as posed,
nor to the sound of partial truth in the making.

Future of our people is spread across the landscapes of The Kingdoms of God,
as denominated by each Nation under God.

Future of our people bears upon the languages learnt at birth,
the education of the young,
the growth lines of the youth,
the maturity of the characters established,
with their accompanying levels of activity:
within their own Freewill.

Future of our people will in part be determined by individual investigations,
by taking trips in groups,
by their intellects being nourished by all
they see and do,
with the ability to comprehend.

Future of our people is borne out by the past,
as survivors of the difficult and seaborne immigrations,
from the days of sail,
unto the installing of the diesels:
with great power and motive force,
in birthing independence from the wind.

Future of our people will no longer be the recipients of setbacks,
the recipients of evil intent,
the recipients of illness and sickness,
as spread about by the careless and the carefree,
where inoculations had no place within the body,
as the germs do grow so bringing harm,
upon the lateness of concern.

Future of our people do not have a future of extinction,
do not have a future bred of global mishaps,
do not have a worry which touches on the abilities of God.

Future of our people is secure and safe,
shall join The Eternal Family of God,
shall arise in the third birth from the grave,
from the sleep of ages,
from the residues restored to be enhanced,
as in The Valley of Dry Bones.

Future of our people can mingle within time,
can select as being out of time,
can remain temporarily or permanently,
within the mortal birthright shell,
of the time sphere of God.

Future of our people can be unrestricted by God.

Future of our people are able to revisit all aspects of presentation of The Earth,
as known to man in his seeking and his travels
down through the ages,
within his timed mortality.

Future of our people can remember and query,
can remember relatives both inside and outside
The Veil of The Bride,
cannot visit nor be known to those outside the veil,
unless among the multitudes—
who pass through The Tribulation
of The Wrath of God,
who settled for respect to so dwell within The Destiny of Default.

Future of our people is not a lonesome lifestyle:
unbounded by friendship and acquaintances,
who seek to know and do.

Future of our people is to experience on a grand scale the habitation of The Earth,
under the rebirth of a new day,
under the transitional grace of My People,
opting for due honouring with powers and senses and abilities,
unencountered in mortality.

Future of our people moves and graduates;
loves and hugs;
sings and praises;
kneels and worships;
learns and appreciates;
assimilates and postulates;
discusses and confirms;
motivates and targets:
the gardening of God.

Future of our people merges into the distance variables as known to God,
merges into Star feasts of invitations,
merges into visits to the very many other orbs of God,
where circling is in progress,
as life is birthed in habitation,
as contact is assured."

My Content Study Aid

____

____

____

Commemoration of A Promise

The End-time Testimonies of God

And I hear God The Father saying,
"Commemoration of a promise should always be as a result of being birthed
into existence,
should always be frequented by the affected,
who have held it in expectation of being honoured,
should always clear any doubts as to standing,
by the dependants and the waiting,
who have heard of it and know.

Commemoration of a promise is initially created by the supposéd trustworthy,
is originally generated in a time frame of the past,
is often forgotten and disposed of as a if a promissory
note forgotten,
to so be overlaid with nought.

Commemoration of a promise signals of success,
signals of a promise kept,
signals of the absence of dissatisfaction.

Commemoration of a promise can come around as if an anniversary,
as if a blending of hope with trust,
as if a positioning in the cold,
where heat cannot be present,
to melt and cause to run away.

Commemoration of a promise vies with the slick as glued to a veneer,
vies with the dishonest who are out for all they can grab,
vies with integrity where choice is put on test,
in comparison with the truth.

Commemoration of a promise seeks and should find the promise,
in its glory still awaiting fulfilment,
in its reservoir of safety,
where none have touched nor contaminated,
its end-time birthing of surprise;
in its being under lock and key,
as the time scale calls for maturity,
of a finger held in readiness.

Commemoration of a promise has polishing in mind,
has an inspection that is as it should be:
where tinkering has not occurred,
with the seals still seen untouched,
with its companions still in place and undisturbed.

Commemoration of a promise upheld can change lives for the better,
as enhancements grow and stretch;
can change lives for the worse,
as the object of affection is pawned and
not recovered,
as someone walks away with the
ignoring of the promise.

Commemoration of a promise can break a heart,
as the promise follows the reality:
of being just a tissue in the water,
from where it starts to fragment;
of being just as a salmon in a stream,
fighting hard to beat the current,
to then become but the meal for
a patient hungry bear;
of being but as a vibration in a wooden hall,
as the revellers jump up and
down in unison,
so freeing to enable the only
bulb to fuse.

Commemoration of a promise satisfies the time of arrival of a setting,
of arrival of a party of like minds,
of arrival of the music makers with their
percussions and their wind,
when all is set and decorated,
for when the promise is brought
forth to be unveiled.

Commemoration of a promise remembers a memory on trial,
a memory which forgets,
a memory that intruded,
with enquiries seeking verification of commitment,
expected but not known.

Commemoration of a promise neither startles nor shames,
neither exaggerates nor diminishes,
neither entwines nor cuts free.

Commemoration of a promise does not test to breakage,
does not stretch unto the strain threshold,
does not dismember nor destroy the hope and truth,
within a promise with accountability,
based on the shoreline of accomplishment with
the striving for success.

Commemoration of a promise is gratified by fulfilment,
is satisfied by completion,
is matured by a target date of failure or of reinstatement.

Commemoration of a promise when suspected to face a likely fracturing prior
to maturity,
should be issued with a proviso of 'God willing'—
the implication being that something may occur,
which would prevent a successful outcome to the promise,
just sought or declared.

Commemoration of a promise encounters interests of children,
where their wanting of a promise,
is based upon past disappointments,
where candidness is not really understood,
where a broken promise carries portents
of untrustworthiness,
as it is often broken without regret,
to never carry the recompense,
for when integrity ensures that the promise is upheld,
is made good to clear the slate of a child's disappointment,
created through the longing to take part,
in an adventure with an adult,
of an excitement appealing to the heart and all which is involved.

Commemoration of a promise should not be made without a qualification:
the promise may not be able to be upheld:
in a specific time frame,
or when placed in vain without due care and attention,
to so be judged as a broken promise,
which turns into an unbecoming lie,
then gathering as a penalty awaiting for fulfilment,
with the destiny of default—
now changed for the prospect of respect,
as honouring is forced to turn its back under direct confrontation,
of non-acceptable failure in the eyes of the young recipient:
as known and marked by God."

My Content Study Aid

Resolution of The Nitpickers

The End-time Testimonies of God

And I hear God The Father saying,
"Resolution of the nitpickers breeds exasperation among their fellows,
terminates with ill feelings,
has no room for existence within The Eternity of God.

Resolution of the nitpickers sees no halos installed,
sees no greeting of any friends,
sees no crowns upon the heads.

Resolution of the nitpickers will remove the fault finders,
who bring nothing new to discussions,
will remove the smug and self-satisfied
from 'the operas' on the street corners,
from 'the sing-songs' in the parks,
from 'the tuneless strumming' and the mediocre voices,
as found upon the sidewalks and the footpaths,
of much convenience to the shoppers and the window gazers,
on perambulations through the centres of a town or city.

Resolution of the nitpickers usually deal with irrelevancies,
usually take them very seriously,
usually are never satisfied with a practical solution.

Resolution of the nitpickers look at everything as if through a microscope,
attend to identifying details not considered perfect,
would call to attention all they have considered,
are expectant of some praise,
fail to understand the immaterial in preventing
much attention,
other than a glance of interruption,
prior to ignoring and continuing.

Resolution of the nitpickers can multiply and spread if left to their own devices,
need to be stamped on and stopped within their tracks,
before dislocation with interruptions become commonplace occurrences,
within a production chain being subjected to their inspections ad nauseam.

Resolution of the nitpickers play a tune all of their own,
keep harping on their findings,
as if being of some importance,
do not understand why their queries are not answered,
why their comments have no standing of
any real significance.

Resolution of the nitpickers are everywhere abounding,
encroach upon the stable and the working,
would upset the applecart from smooth running:
if given half a chance.

Resolution of the nitpickers are not a friendly crowd,
becoming bitter by their treatment,
fail to understand the overview of management,
believe the urgency is not being recognized,
as replacements should be scheduled:
those which would result in little difference,
if any,
as an increase in perceptible performance.

Resolution of the nitpickers do not grow profitability,
do not grow any productivity able to be measured,
do not increase cash flow either in their trials or in
their recommendations.

Resolution of the nitpickers do not like to be ignored,
think they are attaining valuable results,
in drawing attention to what they consider as
a failure of design,
so being in need of an amendment,
which,
from experience,
will not change the status quo.

Resolution of the nitpickers are the plague of the shop stewards,
are the straddlers of management,
are the seekers of forums which are not sympathetic to their
rants and raves.

Resolution of the nitpickers vie with one another,
in abstractions carried to extremes,
carried to measurements no longer seen as meaningful,
carried on the shop floor to anyone who will stop to listen:
to regurgitations of old difficulties long since fixed:
deleted from attention.

Resolution of the nitpickers are the night hawks wandering the corridors,
of mechanical monsters of complexity,
of robots with their shiny faces:
of repetitive actions,
of conveyors of simplicity and complexity:
as they move and sort and stack and pile.

Resolution of the nitpickers see all as their domain,
yet are the guardians of nothing,
are the stickybeaks of industry,
and anything that takes their fancy.

Resolution of the nitpickers interpose opinions when they are not called for,
interpose offers of assistance when they are not needed,
interpose an analysis into every conversation,
where such are destined to be ignored.

Resolution of the nitpickers often bring frustration,
as they chase and tender unsolicited and useless information,
stale and out-of-date areas they consider worth pursuing,
small irrelevant comments as judged to be their moments:
of inspirational concepts,
of value to one and all which they all deserve to hear,
with attention to the fore.

Resolution of the nitpickers,
in the view of others:
are the time wasters par excellence,
are the ones with nothing worth listening to,
as they seek to stop and chat,
are the industrial missionaries without a mission,
are the cockerels of the barnyard which stop to peck at
anything which takes their fancy,
are the naggers and the nuisances,
are the specialists in interruptions,
are the blind and deaf to any form of correction or of input
to their spirits or their souls.

Resolution of the nitpickers achieves no admittance,
to an Eternal destiny of choice as The Committed,
The Testifiers,
within The Would-be-bride of Christ,
where gratitude is missing from a narrowness of mind."

My Content Study Aid

Home Within The Wonderland

The End-time Testimonies of God

And I hear God The Father saying,
"Home within the wonderland is an inspiring place to be,
is an amazing place to wander,
is a superlative place to be able to call home—
after the fulfilment of three births,
after all the days within mortality,
after all the preparation for Eternity,
with a sure path leading home to where it all began.

Home within the wonderland will introduce the onset of adventures,
of discoveries,
of informed opinion,
of wisdom pouring in.

Home within the wonderland opens up the prospects for advancement,
opens up aeons of existence where time is unimportant,
opens up the opportunity to resettle,
to be with a family,
opens up being near to facilities with appeal,
opens up the enjoyment of the selected views,
opens up the comfort attached to relaxation,
where there is no rush nor need to carry.

Home within the wonderland has transport at a beck and call,
has methods all in place,
has needs in readiness to be met without discomfort,
has a way of life where livelihoods can be put at rest or
lived according to a relay of abundance.

Home within the wonderland is not dependent on invitations,
runs on a basis of a 'drop-in' or a 'drop-by',
where friendship is wide spread,
while relatives,
both close and distant,
both known and unknown,
are mostly there within their extensive family trees.

Home within the wonderland is the jumping off point,
to interface with stars:
in all the field time completeness,
of both structure and appearance;
in all the variants in temperature,
atmosphere,

gravity,
and pressure;
with a possible life which may squirt or heave;
where water,
if found,
spreading purposes and applications quite
familiar to The Earthbound.

Home within the wonderland has gateways,
has portals,
has walkways,
has flyways,
has shuttles to the fore,
has controlled movements available to all the extant entities,
to be found in their being in Eternity,
has arrival and departure points,
landing and takeoff facilities,
for those who like to journey;
has transfer and reception areas for the speedy and
the forthright:
where the timing of an instant or a blink,
sees movement both started and completed,
across light years as evidenced within the requests
and desires,
as such surface for attention with completion.

Home within the wonderland always holds the attention for,
and the attendant love of,
being home.

Home within the wonderland always serves up the expectations,
never fails on service,
never pulls the chain on defeat.

Home within the wonderland brings familiarity across what were previously divides;
what was previously a no-go area of conflict;
what was thought to be an area governed
by the snow or ice as capped or buried;
by the desert with the sand or heat as encountered;
by the fuelling of the rivers or the lakes,
where water flows in action or lies at rest,
as gravity is satisfied.

Home within the wonderland has no difficult in satisfying the requests and thoughts,
in alignment with the ambitions,
of those who dwell therein.

Home within the wonderland leaves much within the factors leading to decisions,
leaves much within the 'know how' and the mechanics
of survival,
leaves much within the love and care and oversight of God.

Home within the wonderland is a place where friends do meet,
is a place where everyone feels at home,
unconfined within the freedom of space with distance,
as exists within Eternity.

Home within the wonderland has fluctuating seasons,
has fluctuating availability of travel to the very many stars,
with their siblings as captured bit by bit,
as they are brought into existence
at the creative word of God.

Home within the wonderland has choice in decoration of a dwelling place,
as readied for occupation,
as prepared and put in place,
within the advance promising of God.

Home within the wonderland is a result of careful selection,
of qualifying within the fields of mortal preparation,
of adhering to the requirements of the mouth,
the body and the spirit,
in the counselling of the soul,
as to the use and application of Freewill,
in the commitment and the testimony within
the following of My Son,
in the honouring of My Son,
as sin is forsaken,
as the gifts of The Spirit of My Son are uplifted,
to be so enabled to magnify a life in surroundings,
where holiness is sought.

Home within the wonderland has a future without peer,
has a future which has no fear of reproduction,
has a future where there is no lying,
as truth and righteousness have overcome the negatives,
to so secure sacred opportunities:
as Peace secures the growth of Happiness and Contentment,
within the maturity established for being within
The Eternity with God."

My Content Study Aid

Bounds Within Eternity

The End-time Testimonies of God

And I hear God The Father saying,
"Bounds within Eternity are not imposed by God.

Bounds within Eternity are temporarily sustained by circumstance,
imposed by those who are able to make it so,
for all so selected.

Bounds within Eternity can separate The Sacred and The Secular,
can segregate My People from The Multitudes,
as survivors of The End-time Tribulation.

Bounds within Eternity can expedite and forestall,
can encourage and dismay,
can mystify and disturb,
can succumb in non-belief,
can search the knowledge engines of the universes,
as to why this is so,
as to whether a solution is both tenable and applicable,
as fixation is asserted,
as barriers are imposed.

Bounds within Eternity are safeguards against elitism,
are safeguards against satanic upheaval,
are safeguards against The Multitude seeking power,
and/or authority to self-govern.

Bounds within Eternity are difficult to discern when in place,
are difficult to shift or lift when required,
are difficult to disarm or to neutralize,
when set within a time shield of security.

Bounds within Eternity when set,
do not permit the come and go,
do not permit the call for 'Help',
do not register the call of 'Fire',
when such are initiated by the sensors of the body,
with encodings complete to activate only when assessed,
as in need to summon to assist,
or to remove to a source of skilled endeavour.

Bounds within Eternity are complex and assured,
are thought out and applicable,
are resolute and guarded when accosted by behaviour,
in need of restraint.

Bounds within Eternity are sources of known protection,
are sources which prevent the bypassing of the gates into Eternity,
are the checks and balances ensuring purity and worth are maintained,
in an environment of internationalism,
where fence jumpers do exist and liars do exaggerate,
in efforts to invade or to dispense with,
the creativity of God,
where entry is by invitation only,
as assessments of the applicants are found to have integrity and honour,
in following all The Cross implies and upholds,
as worthy to sustain.

Bounds within Eternity determine the admission of numbers to a site,
so it is not more than be coped with on the day,
determine the shallowness and the density,
in stretching past horizons,
determine the levels of activity with appeals to mercy,
in assurance that justice is not aligned to serve a misapplication,
built and founded on unequal ends.

Bounds within Eternity arise,
ebb,
and flow,
in the securing of the whole of society,
accepted into the growth patterning of Eternity.

Bounds within Eternity maintain the finality of the one-way trips:
arising from the graves;
maintain the segments of the secular from the sacred,
for the multitudes surviving the end-time tribulation experience,
with an ending where the presence of justification on Freewill,
decides the destinies incurred.

Bounds within Eternity can sequence and vanish,
can detail and record,
will neither collapse nor disintegrate.

Bounds within Eternity have vast distances to cover:
when required,
when setup for installation,
when sought out for inspection.

Bounds within Eternity do not stall the travellers in mid-sending,
do not bring down those on intergalactic journeys,
where transition time is very short,
do not impinge on the welfare of those intent on visiting,
or on transits of discovery.

Bounds within Eternity are not ones seeking publicity,
are not ones rigged with alarm bells,
are not ones where people are distraught.

Bounds within Eternity are there for protection and restriction,
are there for a very long long time,
if it were desirable to measure such,
within the guidelines of mortality.

Bounds within Eternity know the limits acceptable to those within An Eternal Kingdom,
encounter little by way of distraction,
encounter less by way of an attempted intrusion,
encounter mostly just the undisturbed qualities,
of the status quo.

Bounds within Eternity rest upon success,
cannot afford a failure or a breach,
ensure all are well,
are operating as they should.

Bounds within Eternity encounter no scenes of idolatry,
no scenes of turmoil arising from frustration,
no scenes of damage or of destruction,
as attached to the crowding of a street,
as now vacated from a suburb of residential homes.

Bounds within Eternity sing the songs of undisturbed solitude,
as encountered at distances from the gates of entry,
from the portals no longer seen to be in use,
as foreseen and prepared for the influx arising:
from within The Truths of Righteousness
and Peace,
from in The Realms of Kings and Queens,
who live and serve the pre-eminence of The King of Kings,
within the nations of the footstool,
in governance with informed and stable advisors,
who know the standards as required,
for what is both safe and just."

My Content Study Aid

Reaching For The Stars

The End-time Testimonies of God

And I hear God The Father saying,
"Reaching for the stars honours all eternity which makes it possible,
simplistic,
as it caters to The Inquisitive now in a situation,
where both time and space are conquered,
in yielding up their secrets,
as evident in their modes of travel.

Reaching for the stars has long been on the mind of man,
when within mortality;
has long been beyond the reach or the reality,
of both the means and the resources,
which were not helped by theory.

Reaching for the stars is the starting of a journey,
is the sating of inborn curiosity,
is the interpretation resulting in a rewarding practicality.

Reaching for the stars opens eyes with the thought flexing of the new found senses
of infinity.

Reaching for the stars opens up the choice,
as darkness of the night is lit up by the interface with space:
where time is seen to rule to so dominate the abilities of man,
to venture off the ground in a meaningful progression,
from where return is assured in accordance,
with the distance as linked to the engineering might of man.

Reaching for the stars confirms the onward aspirations of man,
his ability to devise and to confound,
to develop and to charter,
to wander and return.

Reaching for the stars is the ultimate ministry abroad,
the ultimate pointing to evangelism,
the prospecting for the signatures of other life forms,
where self awareness ensures ongoing survival in their gifted habitations,
which are worlds apart in isolation,
born of an ongoing sense of inability to see or to sense,
across the great distances involved.

Reaching for the stars has the requirement to stipulate the target of the voyage,
the co-ordinates as calculated,
the distances involved which are not measured in light years,

rather they are measured with great accuracy,
in billionths of a second,
which has yet to reach to one,
which has light years speeded up,
as distances are re-interpreted,
within the power house of God.

Reaching for the stars is to be easy and seen as popular,
is to be interesting and seen as encouraging,
is to be worthwhile with effort seen as being rewarding:
in declaring views previously not available to see within mortality.

Reaching for the stars is on offer in Eternity,
is rewarding of preparation,
is available with a Freewill selection choice of a destiny of honour.

Reaching for the stars arises from the releasing from The Cross,
arises from the reconciliation of The Cross,
arises from the shadows of The Cross:
as they come alive for evermore.

Reaching for the stars can show stars of selection:
where zooming is optional,
with self-focussing for clarity.

Reaching for the stars are not inhibited by distance,
are not inhibited by survivability,
are neither inhibited by temperature nor by gravity.

Reaching for the stars opens eyes in wonder at the variations in design,
at the landfalls as envisaged,
at the descriptive summaries as available
for knowledge impartation.

Reaching for the stars can utilize journeys which can be lengthened or shortened,
which can be oval with no stops,
or destination projected with an all inclusive built-in return.

Reaching for the stars is not a visit to the candy store,
is not a visit to an adventure playground,
is not as if on a bus,
where The Stop is waiting to be called or to have a button pressed.

Reaching for the stars can be of singular simplicity or of multiple complexity.

Reaching for the stars may have items overlooked,
or segments expressing understanding,
may seem inviting for a touch down,
without the knowledge of the background status,
nor of the expectations of all to be encountered.

Reaching for the stars are flyby's at the best,
where closeness is controlled,
are not holiday camps in the sky,
for frolicking and racing on the surface as presented.

Reaching for the stars can offer passing closeups:
to increase appreciation of the scenery,
can draw attention to the landscapes and the surfaces,
as they come and go,
with memories established for retelling,
when groups are reunited with descriptions then abounding.

Reaching for the stars brings contentment with success,
brings laughter with satisfaction,
brings certainty of belief for specific hot spots,
to validate in confirmation,
where all have been and seen the marvels,
together with the liked and frowned on,
and especially so the oddballs:
needing to be seen to be believed;
all as now known to be dwelling in deep space,
to be far beyond the mortal reach of man.

Reaching for the stars demonstrate the creation activity of our God,
holds up for examination that where He has been and done,
where He has been and is continuing,
where He is and is yet to start.

Reaching for the stars teaches and instructs of the creation power,
authority,
and planning ability:
of all which is on nightly display,
amid the wonders of the heavens,
from the spoken words of God."

My Content Study Aid

Meeting With The Neighbours

The End-time Testimonies of God

And I hear God The Father saying,
"Meeting with the neighbours can be a testing of individual preparation,
can be a testing of commitment as a follower,
as a disciple,
as a lip server in The Multitudes.

Meeting with the neighbours is a testing place for My second commandment,
is a consolidator of approach with understanding of position,
is the seeking of a friendship which may reach unto the stars.

Meeting with the neighbours should not settle on a casual relationship,
should grow and develop as like outlooks,
with their interests,
are discovered and expanded.

Meeting with the neighbours is not a matter of the rights and wrongs,
is more a matter of their walks into eternity,
with a sincere appreciation for Righteousness with Truth,
where support of both the trials and the successes,
uplift both the neighbours and their families,
into the arena of affirmation of both belief with Faith and Will,
in characters developing within the aspects as sheltered,
by Freewill within The Freedom of release:
where accountability oversees intent.

Meeting with the neighbours can have life changing ramifications,
can bring solitude out from within a cabinet,
can bring surliness to be placed within a dustbin,
can establish to the fore that which carries on behind.

Meeting with the neighbours has many areas of conversation,
of interests and of hobbies,
of both games at home and
of sports upon the battle fields of play.

Meeting with the neighbours decries the need to shout,
decries the need to envy,
decries the need for comparisons of acquisitions
when to the fore,
when opened to discussions.

Meeting with the neighbours is often a time to share,
a time to offer assistance or of help,
a time to verify good health,

a time to evaluate the problems,
a time to reason with the difficulties,
a time to pray for the things that only God can fix,
or call up for attention.

Meeting with the neighbours has a discussion time for the goals in life,
of how to set objectives,
of why to toe the line,
of when to recuperate from all that illness has delivered.

Meeting with the neighbours is not a route to the vanquishing of evil,
is not a route to assured success in gathering wealth,
is not a recipe for leaning on the shoulders,
is not the permission grounds for spreading lies
or defamation.

Meeting with the neighbours opens opportunities for discussing wisdom:
of how it may be acquired;
for settling on the family holiday;
for arriving at the way open to retirement;
for examining the funding and the counting of expenses;
for the means of the extending of life expectancy,
for when grandchildren are active in surroundings.

Meeting with the neighbours varies with suggestions,
varies with the planning,
varies with the numbers,
varies with the destination,
varies with the time limit,
with the travelling involved.

Meeting with the neighbours can include entertainment and activities,
as suitable for the participants,
as suitable for the locality,
as dependent on resources as available,
whether bounded by the sea,
the lakes,
the snow fields,
the skating ponds,
or playgrounds of a resort or city
with some parks.

Meeting with the neighbours can include a time for meals,
with a setting seen as both attractive and affordable,
when children have their interest held,
where focus can be on the unusual with surprises,
in the meeting of the expectations of both adults and the children.

Meeting with the neighbours can see the spending:
of a successful day well spent,
of rides upon a train as it goes back and forth,
of going on a bus trip,
of experiencing a fishing rod and reel,
of swimming on a lake shore,
of bathing in a wilderness where hot water gushes forth,
of sliding down a luge where the landscape tends to blur,
of climbing up a hill where puffing attends the fastest,
of photographing animals as seen within a zoo,
of flying a kite as prepared for a windy day,
of visiting a field where model planes do fly and zoom,
of stopping on a river bank to unpack a picnic,
where the banks do hide the tunnelled nests,
of those who know how to fish,
to so gather for their young,
who have been told not to attract attention,
when they are left alone,
having been entrusted to stay within the
confines of the nest,
until their feathers have extended,
until they are invited by their parents to explore,
all that is found at the end of the tunnel,
where the light does dwell,
as it beckons timid minds.

Meeting with the neighbours does not have to be limited to soup and toast,
can be a time of stretching the imagination,
of having the courage to elope into the sunshine of the day,
of wearing a smile all day long with both joy and glee,
at all that is for the eyes to see and the ears to hear,
in attending,
for the first observant time,
the creativity of God:
as butterflies are seen to flit and bounce upon their wings,
as the birds and trees are singing,
their own songs of Faith in The Sonlight,
of Grace in God's Wind."

My Content Study Aid

Encountering The Shuttles

The End-time Testimonies of God

And I hear God The Father saying,
"Encountering the shuttles brings travelling to the fore,
brings travelling into consideration,
brings travelling into the hows and whens and whys.

Encountering the shuttles speak of two-part departures,
speak of two-part returns,
speak of more than two when transport is required,
to link multiple stopovers as requested in the routing,
when they fly the routes through space,
without the instantaneous transits where viewing on the highways,
declares neither proof nor sign of movement.

Encountering the shuttles are the introductory means of moving,
The Transients into the surroundings of the relay stations of The Lord,
into the co-ordinated of both front and rear,
into the high speed transducers,
the super signallers of fore and aft,
the impulse generators that create the preparatory
phase from where matter is excluded,
from where matter is described in
dimensions as required,
where massless information only
is converted,
as the key to instant movement,
as mass is left behind,
as mass is regenerated at the point of arrival,
as the information based instructions are
interpreted and read,
as set to recreate an existence in the distant setting,
to deflect the traveller's bodily mass from
his intended destination,
as information is transferred between the
heart beats,
in readiness for reproducing,
where the heart does not miss a beat,
and life continues as before.

Encountering the shuttles occurs as a matter of course in the sequences within
entity relocations.

Encountering the shuttles occasions the necessary connectivity,
to maintain the white-hole linkages,
across the space continuum:
where 'black-holes' are a misnomer as light exists,
within the force fields as engaged.

Encountering the shuttles can be a grand surprise,
can be an unexpected arrival,
can be a sharing of conditions,
together with the destinies as programmed.

Encountering the shuttles is not a scene of urgency,
is a scene of scheduling,
is a place where shuttles stop to wait,
is a station where the shuttles linger for awhile:
as the schedules are updated,
as the passengers are checked for acceptance,
with the travel knowledge base intact,
as readied for the journeys now to be in hand.

Encountering the shuttles is not to be taken as evidence of an impending travelogue,
is not to be assumed that travelling is the occupier of the mind,
is not to be taken as a given that the shuttles will not cancel,
to reverse proposals neither confirmed nor accepted on a schedule.

Encountering the shuttles does not place toys before an engineer,
does not indicate a proposition for a trial,
does not require fumigation when entry is not made.

Encountering the shuttles showcases the loading of the committed,
the loading of the capsules,
the segregating of the age groups with their various interests,
the equipping with the clothing as deemed to be advisable,
the end-limiting of capacity commensurate with size,
as preparation is completed to progress to the impulse generators,
and so unto conversion.

Encountering the shuttles is both the starting point and the ending point,
of travel composure within the star-fields of the galaxies,
awaits until the shuttles are no longer being used,
where freedom is recovered with the memories,
as the senses become information gatherers and storers,
of all that is encountered within the stars belts,
throughout the skies of God.

Encountering the shuttles creates interest in appearance,
as enhanced by slick of form and of presentation,
of silence and of being sealed within the windowless,
and the escape proof as a short countdown,
pre-empts the proximity of the coming floating ionisation,
without a sense of gravity,
or the need for boosting from non-existent rockets.

Encountering the shuttles are not the rocket ships as when in mortality,
rather they are consistent with the need for faster means of travel,
where distances are much greater,
where time no longer is the basis of a habitual problem,
when within the time sphere of man now transmuted,
to the gravity waves of God.

Encountering the shuttles for the first time,
can be an awe filled experience,
or a frightening one,
where everything is different and application of the instruments,
in the automatic mode,
are far from clear as to the functioning,
or enabling any form of simplistic understanding.

Encountering the shuttles is a test of will,
when repeat transfers are suggested,
or sought within the capability of the pods concerned.

Encountering the shuttles are not of what dreams are built when within mortality,
are the crossovers for the reaching of the stars,
are the subsuming of simplicity,
are the results of infinite design,
where wisdom of the ages qualifies perfection,
established among the marvels of eternity,
as God oversees all that is both good and capable,
of achieving all that is required,
within the spoken Word of God."

My Content Study Aid

Coping with The Scale and Scope

The End-time Testimonies of God

And I hear God The Father saying,
"Coping with the scale and scope as they march up and down the drawing boards,
pose a problem for those who cannot envisage,
for those who cannot picture that which awaits development,
for those who cannot segregate the components of the tableau,
as each measures up to both the site and the location.

Coping with the scale and scope is a tribute to imagination,
is a tribute as to how all fits together,
is a tribute as to meaning and interpretation.

Coping with the scale and scope does neglect the colour wheel of man,
does not neglect the colour palette of God,
as the colours shift and blend among the stars,
as the colours create the raptures and the marvels,
as the curtains bow and curtsey with the orchestras
in tune,
with precision in starting,
in completing,
right on key.

Coping with the scale and scope sees miniatures and goliaths intermingled,
on the site plans of Eternity,
as they rear and ambulate across the areas,
where footprints are quite obvious that something
very large,
or very small both have the right to existence,
as each makes its way through surroundings,
in which lifestyles are created and maintained.

Coping with the scale and scope is a measurer's greatest joy,
sees enthusiasm expressed,
sees enlargements considered,
sees suppositions mixing with possibilities,
sees the finished forms of life merging into the present,
as fitted for the future.

Coping with the scale and scope may not be immediately obvious as to exactly what,
the adopted parameters will yield,
may require corrections to assumptions,
may seek more leeway in the games of hide and seek,
may require more allowances for aspects of
the environment,
may require consideration as to how and when the water
flows over a projected landscape,
so it may be able to sustain the drinking requirements
of all who call it home,
or for those who are simply visitors in transit.

Coping with the scale and scope requires a great deal of thought and conjecture,
requires a great deal of experience and capability,
requires a great deal of patience and consideration—
so all may be thrilled within their newly found freedom,
where both size and appetite are settled with satisfaction
as befits one and all.

Coping with the scale and scope requires initial supervision,
to verify the practicality of the standards,
as set for performance parameters,
across a whole and complete widespread environment,
where prey and predator need to be intermingled,
within the feeding chain which is able to support,
and so to maintain the diversity required.

Coping with the scale and scope sets the standards for maturity,
where hunting is the game,
with the end result one of selective death.

Coping with the scale and scope is an ambitious step,
best left to the care and knowledge base of God.

Coping with the scale and scope is not an aspect,
of the planet's management best left to man,
for history has a record of the fearsome stick,
as wielded by man in his search for gain,
both from the seas and from the land,
has not in any way been considerate on species,
who could not prevent the prolonged attacks,
which eventually also killed the last remaining groups,
to add them to the extinction list as a result of plundering and robbing,
with neither care nor respect for the boundaries,
decided as a means of protection,
wherein the poachers still killed and created orphans without regard
for anything:

with the only interest being the looting of reserves,
both on the land and in the seas,
as their greed to fill their purses witnessed:
how that and scarcity forced what they deemed marketable,
into the horrors of being slaughtered to extinction.

Coping with the scale and scope of the blood-shed,
in the so called 'wild',
are seen to threaten almost every living thing,
found to be of commercial value to man,
somewhere on The Earth.

Coping with the scale and scope beggars belief,
when one sees how disregard for protection for the native species,
by the native people,
has a history of extortion of the assets,
whether in the forests or chased across the plains,
as their numbers continue to decline,
so bordering on irrecoverability,
in expressing a complete lack of care,
for the welfare,
of those which are supposed to be under care and protected,
as native species where jungles are attacked,
as everything is laid to waste and environments destroyed,
as slash and burn is rampant,
as living space is captured,
as there is no longer any space:
where the jungle dwellers are able to call 'home'.

Coping with the scale and scope will soon witness,
the scale and scope as portrayed,
as in need of being,
under the active management of God."

My Content Study Aid

Justice Sought and Rendered

The End-time Testimonies of God

And I hear God The Father saying,
"Justice sought and rendered without full and honest knowledge,
will spread injustice wide and far,
for where an appeal is called,
with integrity of testimony.

Justice sought and rendered is not likely to be consistent within the mortality of man,
is certain to be consistent within The Eternity of God.

Justice sought and rendered speaks as if apples in a box,
where all are similar and consistent,
as a path is followed leading back and forth.

Justice sought and rendered does not affect the colour of the fruit,
does not affect its usefulness or taste,
does not affect the numbers on the tree:
once the tree has set the crop in expectation,
with the codlin moths kept well at bay.

Justice sought and rendered requires equality before the law,
requires similar penalties for similar misdemeanours,
requires similar setbacks for similar infractions.

Justice sought and rendered is not a function of the weather,
is not a function of the time,
is not a function of the visitors,
as seated in the courtrooms in readiness,
of the proceedings as are scheduled for the day.

Justice sought and rendered speaks of promptness in finality,
speaks of promptness in delivery,
speaks of the sincerity of testimony with the courtrooms'
emphasis on Truth:
as the vowed and sworn are heard,
as conflicts are resolved,
as hesitation is dissolved.

Justice sought and rendered brings Truth begging for a hearing,
cries out for an injustice where obstinance prevails,
yet sense remains obtuse and crying out,
for a backtracking only partially resolves the matters
still outstanding,
as they await full resolution.

Justice sought and rendered are matters sometimes very complex,
where past testimony has not been helpful,
and the mire still clings to the post,
where it was at its thickest in waiting to be shed.

Justice sought and rendered will be as stipulated,
before the officers of the court,
will be as testified in validation,
where Truth is at its peak,
will be as recorded where Truth flares off the pages,
as impelled by common sense with the wisdom of the shepherd's dog:
who guards and watches over the attitudes of the sheep,
as they are gathered for the night,
with their Faith so placed in Trust.

Justice sought and rendered stops short at the path,
as built on make believe,
has a red light blinking at the early skittish skids,
has the green light confirming Truth,
which does not falter in the telling,
having no telltale marks of exaggeration,
with blushes on the cheeks.

Justice sought and rendered has promptness in the closing,
has promptness in the dealing,
with the consequences as occurring in the law,
has promptness with the qualifiers and the certifiers,
in winding up the statements,
in the composing of the records as understood and found,
as to where justice takes a walk within a 'wild'
park on the green,
where the oak still had no leaves,
as spring is still to welcome the farewelling,
of the climate with the snow.

Justice sought and rendered leaves no bitterness,
upon the tongue,
leaves no surliness in defeat,
leaves no jubilation at another's loss,
and a frozen mandate to act further as had happened before.

Justice sought and rendered is simplistic to behold,
is a new certification of The Truth,
with the variance as heard within the past,
now discarded and disqualified where the harm is ended,
and The Truth propels the modified present into the future:
where it should have always rightly been.

Justice sought and rendered is sometimes seen as a catchup from the past;
is sometimes seen as an enlargement of the present;
is sometimes seen as what was once an empty vacuum,
now pumping as it fills to overflowing,
the once lost,
but now regained,
rewards for effort and achievement.

Justice sought and rendered often follow one another,
where the sounds are flat and cold,
where the sounds are dim and echoing,
where the sounds do not ring loud and true.

Justice sought and rendered often are the echoers of two negatives,
often are the lapsing of both Hope and Truth,
often are the results of lies as found within the coaxing,
of the devil.

Justice sought and rendered needs to be pursued,
while the light is green,
needs to have the trials surmounted and mastered,
in readiness for the corrective day in court.

Justice sought and rendered will not go unanswered,
when a need cries out for justice,
which has been deposed,
by the liars and the deceitful who would proclaim the 'not' rather than the 'is'.

Justice sought and rendered brings justice to the blind,
brings justice to the deaf,
brings justice to the broke and the forlorn,
brings justice to the distant and the harried,
brings justice to a new platform where the liars and the
cheats had thought they'd won the day.

For as Justice calls so Satan is dispelled.

For as Righteousness is rendered so faces are seen to smile with joy.

For as the new beginnings dawn so the dust is swept away—
to not be invited to return."

My Content Study Aid

___

___

___

Selecting in The Present

The End-time Testimonies of God

And I hear God The Father saying,
"Selecting in the present is a present from the past.
Selecting in the present is a present from the future.

Selecting in the present is the ways and means reserved for travelling,
outside the time frame of the present,
where the past has priority,
where the future is more difficult as it depends
upon the happenings,
between the here and then.

Selecting in the present is quite different,
when the time sphere of man in his mortality is removed,
as ageing is stopped in its tracks,
as tomorrow never comes,
as yesterday never is renewed,
as there is neither progression through the day,
nor the occurrence of the night.

Selecting in the present speaks of immediacy of action,
speaks of the circular of intent,
speaks of the resolution of revolving synchronicity.

Selecting in the present cannot harpoon the past,
nor relegate it further;
cannot entrap the future,
nor draw it to a close.

Selecting in the present gives a myriad of instantaneity,
gives a surplus of immediate choice,
imposes thought transfer as the means of comprehension,
which is fast enough to be decisive,
when commissioning without delay.

Selecting in the present does not pick up the frog croaking in the pond,
does not pick up the sound of traffic roaring to its destiny,
does not pick up the mobile from the static.

Selecting in the present does not drape a flag,
cannot hurry in a turmoil,
can neither secrete nor hide.

Selecting in the present is presented when selecting in dimensions,
where time is non-existent.

Selecting in the present is a strange place to be,
is a place where things are not as they seem,
where motion may not be a blessing,
may be more of a hindrance,
as observation may deny The Truth,
of what the eyes do really see,
in the reporting of the facts.

Selecting in the present should not be undertaken,
without tuition as to expectation,
without tuition as to how to enter,
and as to how to leave,
for returning to the familiar conditions:
in which life is lived to be sustained on a
social basis.

Selecting in the present is a quirkiness of zipping out of the time shield,
because of astounding speed,
which exceeds the ability of time to record the passing,
of what might be assumed to be reality in motion.

Selecting in the present witnesses sound being left behind as speed increases,
so can 'time' and 'light' be left behind,
as the traveller surpasses the speed at which these two can travel,
through the surrounding environment,
yet cannot catch the traveller in a new entity of existence,
where mass no longer is contained.

Selecting in the present can only be achieved within the overriding canopy of God,
where He does arrange the starting and the endpoints,
of an entity travelling outside the existence,
of the daily norm with no recollection,
except the noticing of the overall passing of time
within reality,
as absence of the entity,
has no record of the happenings,
while in the process of the driving of a car.

Selecting in the present introduces the absence of entity,
the cognitive functions put on hold,
the ability to initiate,
to avoid,
and to stop,
no longer held in physical reserve of conscious action.

Selecting in the present does not cause vibrations,
does not bring bouts of nervousness,
does not create fear as to what may result or befall.

Selecting in the present requires amplitude within the mind force,
requires consistency of procession,
requires a replacement oversight for the forsaking of
conscious control,
as handed over to an entity where consciousness is missing,
yet the journey is continuing.

Selecting in the present tests mental stability,
tests uncertainty of attainment,
tests what one would imagine as both dangerous and suicidal,
in travelling a road at 70 kph with its bends and curves,
with a village as placed halfway into the scene.

Selecting in the present is known to God,
is attended by God,
is guarded by God,
so there is no queue which leads to harm or mishap,
under the participation of a schedule as described.

Selecting in the present hears neither horns nor shouts,
encounters no situations where avoidance is not possible
at the speed enjoined,
or as the road is cleared.

Selecting in the present has matters under the care of God,
for the attaining of experience,
has matters supervised by the conscious over the disengaged,
has matters with responders to the fore,
able to control and to maintain the positioning of a car,
as it travels on a road so skinned with bitumen.

Selecting in the present is a victory cry in process,
is a summation of the possible,
is the achieving of the unnerving,
is the encouragement for the achievements of the future,
where brainwaves exercise control without reflection,
on any being other than the loosed authority to God."

My Content Study Aid

Truth and Exaggeration

The End-time Testimonies of God

And I hear God The Father saying,
"Truth and exaggeration are the archetypes of integrity and deceit,
are the expressions bringing light,
are the catch points weaving their hooks into the presenting of Freewill,
are the expositories of Righteousness,
are the boundaries where darkness begins to hide its clothing for the day.

Truth and exaggeration do not succumb to one another,
are irreconcilable,
are enemies at war within the field of words.

Truth and exaggeration are not friends at ease within one another's presence,
are neither compatible in their thought patterning nor in their applications.

Truth and exaggeration are not seen lingering together,
as one is seen both clean and tidy where it dwells in its existence,
while the other is both ragged and messy,
as it litters over its home base,
to strew falseness far and wide.

Truth and exaggeration sees Truth being told only once,
sees exaggeration growing daily as it spreads,
in the absence of a conscience.

Truth and exaggeration are not the super-clashers of reciprocal denials,
where truth has no need for a defence,
while exaggeration is able to be trimmed.

Truth and exaggeration are not mergers of their meanings,
are not equalisers of dissent,
are not the instigators of conflicting results where variance is important.

Truth and exaggeration has the first destined to stand,
so to be supported by the facts,
the second is far from sure of its ground,
may vibrate with its nervousness in defending a deep attack,
which strikes right at the core of definition.

Truth and exaggeration can be taken as the well springs of idle conversation,
where exaggeration bears the brunt of being portrayed as desired,
rather than having extended the weak,
but complimentary aspects of The Truth.

Truth and exaggeration are not friends in the same household,
are not friends when seated at a table,
are not friends when recounting activities:
such as a golfing afternoon where a score is slightly lowered,
or a fishing expedition on a lake,
where the fish become heavier,
as the journey home nears completion,
or a mobile phone comes into use.

Truth and exaggeration,
with the latter under correction,
can destroy an element of Trust,
can bring doubt into what was once a sunny afternoon,
can echo in the halls of immaturity,
as weight and count become downsized,
past the reality of what is actually the case,
and rightly so,
as scepticism takes hold,
where blinks may bring suspicions,
from a face which turns away,
with a mumble put in place.

Truth and exaggeration are sometimes linked together in a situation to impress,
are sometimes offered up to increase a day's success,
are sometimes increased to carry more weight than justified,
are sometimes just a source of excitement running wild.

Truth and exaggeration are not necessarily handmaidens which always fit together,
should not be the instigators of congratulations for success,
should not be bound to the offering of a meal,
should not be a functioning of size when the gutting knife is still
to be applied.

Truth and exaggeration are best kept separated at an arms length,
are best announced with a humble voice,
are best reserved for when Truth has been recovered,
as exaggeration fades back to the reality of the day,
where hopes and expectations do not shower down,
as false and underserved.

Truth and exaggeration can both come into play,
where a weighing-in table discloses the rights and wrongs,
to the over-jubilant and the hopeful,
to the successful and the experienced,
where the scales declare The Truth,
either to dismay or to pride.

Truth and exaggeration will bring their own reward—
to Truth there is both success and reward in alignment with the scales,
to exaggeration are the near tears of disappointment,
as the scales cut down the excess added on in hope.

Truth and exaggeration should not be linked together in a life,
should be treated in isolation to one another,
where Truth should need no fallback position,
so just stands and stands and stands,
while an exaggeration
can expand or contract with the temperature,
can shrink or expand with the icicles of frost,
can revel and dwell when within the temperature of the sea,
or the distance on a road as aligned with a destination.

Truth and exaggeration are crystal clear for the followers of God,
are crystal clear for the outcome of discussions,
are crystal clear when within The Edifice of God,
wherein His people gather in activities,
or for a time of rest.

Truth and exaggeration should not be intermixed,
as both destroy the other when mixing does occur,
as the purity of Truth cannot be easily recovered,
with any certainty from the lot of exaggeration."

My Content Study Aid

Life in a Continuum

The End-time Testimonies of God

And I hear God The Father saying,
"Life in a continuum varies with the strain,
varies with the volatility of change,
varies with the synopsis of what both comes and goes.

Life in a continuum is like living in a melting pot,
is like mixing up the curds,
is like draining off the whey,
is like squeezing on the cheese.

Life in a continuum continues on and on,
has no stop-off point with an opening of escape,
has no startup point where the rumble does commence.

Life in a continuum imprisons its workforce,
as it throws the shuttle back and forth,
as it interleaves the cleft and warp,
as The Jenny does its thing both through the day and through
the night.

Life in a continuum sees the attending of a robotic workforce,
sees the attending of robotic mechanics,
as The Spinning Jenny spins with all spindles put to use,
so the looms do weave,
so the belts do drive.

Life in a continuum develops upwards through time,
as cars are shed like pieces of confetti,
to be spread both far and wide;
as belts are built and driven for the machines of yesteryear.

Life in a continuum bears the frown upon a face,
suffers the scowl as it joins in.

Life in a continuum speaks of boredom to be carried on,
to an end where the beginning is long forgotten,
where achievement is distorted by the lack of pride.

Life in a continuum can waken up a crowd,
can set the tongues a-flapping,
can instill the words of God.

Life in a continuum has church held on a Sunday,
has the bakehouse being made ready to produce,
has the servants bustling here and there with their milk and eggs.

Life in a continuum sees markets to the fore,
sees merchandise on offer,
sees glassware being multiplied.

Life in a continuum is interrupted by the world at war,
by the world with death and mayhem,
by the world with disease and friction,
as it struggles back and forth,
with no leeway for success.

Life in a continuum seeks its measures of success,
its lowering of costs,
its more efficient use of staff.

Life in a continuum can watch the speeding cars,
can watch the games of chance,
can seek the takeoff of burning rubber.

Life in a continuum watches the wall of death,
postulates the ending,
where momentum is the main stay,
which holds everything in order.

Life in a continuum continues with the speed increasing,
continues with the livelihood of youth on two wheeled machines,
with a lot of power and grip.

Life in a continuum sees a continuum to the fore,
sees the milking night and morning,
as the cows queue up in wisdom,
as cycles are repeated to benefit the cows,
and to the man who owns the shed,
which benefit all who enter in.

Life in a continuum illustrates the morning drop offs at a school,
the pickups in the afternoons,
within the ever present cycling of man.

Life in a continuum requires the power to drive,
requires the power to assist and to supply,
requires the power to feed the linked up grid,
with sufficient energy to overcome the static,
and with that as flowing freely to fulfil the end in sight.

Life in a continuum does not stop and fragment,
does not stall in action with a cut out bearing power.

Life in a continuum continues with the turning of the turf,
as the fields are crossed and realigned,
as power is reapplied with all that is required.

Life in a continuum arouses the present in correction.

Life in a continuum selects the motive force with power,
varies with the strength of purpose,
sorts out the muscle from the flab.

Life in a continuum surrounds death with life.
Life in a continuum wakes up the steadfast and concerned.
Life in a continuum leads into the star fields born of residence.

Life in a continuum dwells among survivors,
sequences all the numbers;
gathers all the primes.

Life in a continuum hatches all the numbers seen bearing on a problem.

Life in a continuum musters all the abilities of life,
segregates those found to be in error with the corrected ones concerned.

Life in a continuum continues to infinity,
continues to the pear drop,
continues in the seeking of the message as it is permitted to role forth.

Life in a continuum varies both in majesty and size,
varies both in concept and in gut wrenching with the moisture,
varies with the semblance of the cut,
varies with positiveness of the strike and the posture for forgiveness.

Life in a continuum searches for the best,
searches for what is left,
searches what is best for the filling of a gap.

Life in a continuum reaches for the champion,
who can stand and not be seen to shake.

Life in a continuum evaporates as it disseminates,
rescinds as it proclaims,
declines as it rejects,
whistles as it works,
within the field of give and take,
as it adds up all the labour tasks at hand,
within the care of God."

My Content Study Aid

Appendix

My Content Study Aid

Journaling & Study Notes (1)

Journaling & Study Notes (2)

Journaling & Study Notes (3)

Journaling & Study Notes (4)

Journaling & Study Notes (5)

Journaling & Study Notes (6)

About The Scribe

Updated 16th March 2020

Anthony is 79, having been married to his wife, Adrienne, for 56 years. They have five married children: Carolyn, Alan, Marie, Emma and Sarah and fourteen grandchildren: Matthew & Ella; Phillipa & Jonathan; Jeremy, Ngaire & Trevor; Jake, Finn, Crystal & Caleb; Bjorn, Greta & Minka.

Anthony was raised on a dairy farm in Springston, Canterbury, NZ in the 1940s. He graduated from Canterbury University, Christchurch, NZ with a B.Sc. in chemistry and mathematics in 1962. He was initially employed as an industrial chemist in flour milling and linear programming applications.

These used the first IBM 360 at the university for determining least cost stock food formulations and production parameters. Later he was involved in similar applications on the refining side of the oil industry in Britain, Australia and New Zealand. This was followed by sales and managerial experience in the chemical industry.

The family moved to a Bay of Plenty, NZ, town in 1976 when Anthony took up funeral directing, as a principal, expanding an initial sibling partnership until the close of the century. Anthony acquired practical experience in accounting, business management, and computer usage (early Apples— including The Lisa).

Upon retiring from active funeral directing in 2000 and selling his interests, he then commenced the promotion and the writing of funeral management software for the NZ funeral environment. Rewarded with national success in NZ, with his son also expanding recently into Australia, he has now retired, in 2007, from the active management of that interest, as he quits it entirely in 2020. He lives near some of his family in Hamilton NZ.

Anthony was brought up in the Methodism of his father until his mid-teens, his mother's side was Open Brethren. He is Christian in belief within an Apostolic Pentecostal Charismatic framework of choice (since the 1990s) having been earlier in the Mormon church for several years. Thereafter he was in the Baptist denomination followed by finding a home within the NZ Apostolic (Acts) church movement.

He and his wife, who has visited a number of Asian countries, have been to India in 2011, 12, 13, 16 and 18 on The Lord's tasks and have witnessed and participated in many miracles which befall His People and The Multitudes.

His forbears William Henry Eddy and Margaret Jane Eddy, née Oats, emigrated to New Zealand from Gulval, Cornwall, England in 1878 on a sailing ship, with a very slow passage time of 79 days, and with their three month old infant child, Margaret Anne, dying 21 October 1878 from Congestion of the brain on board the Marlborough while en route to NZ. The Marlborough sailed London 19 September 1878, via Plymouth 26 September 1878, and arrived Lyttelton 14 December 1878 with 336 assisted immigrants. His grandfather, Alfred Charles Eddy, then but three years old, together with an older brother aged four, obviously survived the trials of the sea voyage to become a part of a family with a further eleven New Zealand born siblings all living to maturity.

The 9 Books of either The End-time Psalms of God* or as The End-time Homilies of God

	Pages	Total Words
1. GOD Speaks of Return and Bannered	418	90,840
2. GOD Speaks to Man on The Internet	498	126,434
3. GOD Speaks as His Spirit Empowers	272	68,205
4. GOD Speaks to Man in The End-time	248	62,358
5. GOD Speaks in Letters of Eternity	236	57,644
6. GOD Speaks to His Bridal Presence	326	78,183
7. GOD Speaks to His Edifice	512	126,884
8. GOD Speaks of Loving His Creation	280	71,115
9. GOD Speaks Now of a Seal Revealed	124	24,562

Scribal Note: **These may probably be better known by man in his naming as 'The End-time Homilies of God - in being 'Religious discourses which are intended primarily for spiritual education rather than doctrinal instructions'.*

My Content Study Aid`

The 4 Companion Books of The End-time Flowers of God

	Pages	Total Words
10. GOD End-time Updates Ancient Alien History	310	84,011
11. GOD End-time Updates His Call to The Multitudes	166	46,110
12. GOD End-time Updates The Bride of My Son	180	47,409
13. GOD End-time Updates The Guardianship of Friends	280	82,610

My Content Study Aid`

4 Synopses of The End-time Flowers of God

Book Ten 'God End-time Updates Ancient Alien History' delves into the distant past of Flying Saucers with Alien strangers cross- and interbreeding to generate Neanderthals, and where the discovered new element of Moscovium disintegrates over time into an antigravity fuel, which enables flying saucers to fly the way they do, and where ancient knowledge tells of the extermination of the dinosaurs because of being predators. The current situation, with crop circles and Flying Saucers with real live Aliens, brings history up to date.

Book Eleven 'God End-time Updates His Call to The Multitudes' here The Lord Jesus speaks throughout The Earth— to all who would prepare for an ongoing life with Him. He is reaching out to have The Multitudes come to an understanding and awaits a response in answer to the question of the thoughtful: Why is The Freewill of man of such importance to God? Why is The Freewill of man such a determinant of the ultimate destiny of man? Why is The Freewill of man either respected or honoured by God? Why is The Freewill of man 'Honoured' by his movements within the new covenant?

Book Twelve 'God End-time Updates The Bride of My Son' as dictated by The Father. The Father loves and enfolds as He chooses to bring before The People of The Lord all those who are close to His Heart especially as the wisdom of the centuries has been nurtured in the heavens, is often obvious when spoken, raises eyebrows at the thoughts revealed, silences while matters are considered as to the best way forward. The wisdom of the centuries is a gift from God, is an enlightening of speech, is the victory of expression. The wisdom of the centuries is an expansion of vocabulary.

Book Thirteen 'God End-time Updates The Guardianship of Friends' with eighty six divinely selected scrolls dictated by Jesus: where The Curtain Call of God stimulates: in growth, in Faith, in righteousness, in expression, in quests, in being friendly and inviting. It affirms the value: of being under The Faith Field of Mortality, the confirmation of The Righteous Field of Morality, the requested availability of The Cleansing Field of Grace, the necessity of Seeking The Field of Preparation, The gifts of My Spirit as on The Day of Pentecost, the benefit of attaining fluency in The Heavenly Gift of Tongues, access to the given opportunity to select: the destiny of choice as the goal of life, to be so set in Faith for Freewill Activities— with righteousness prevailing as the destiny is assured. It closes out the time of Grace, opens up the time of Mercy at The Bema Seat.

www.ingramcontent.com/pod-product-compliance
Lightning Source LLC
Chambersburg PA
CBHW072013110526
44592CB00012B/1285
9781950596294